Amelias
compendium of
fashion illustration

featuring the very best in ethical fashion design

published by Amelias House

Dear Reader,

Since 2004 both fashion and illustration have been a strong focus of Amelia's Magazine. Nowadays, we also concentrate on promoting the best in ethical fashion design. So it was only natural for my second book to focus on fashion illustration and ethical fashion.

From an open brief that was posted on my website I chose thirty bright new fashion illustrators to appear in this book; my criteria were creative talent alongside a strong commitment to promotional networking. All of them maintain professional websites and regularly updated blogs, actively participate in social networking and contribute regularly to Amelia's Magazine. In a tough creative world it's absolutely imperative that illustrators get online and find ways to engage with others, and I am very proud that Amelia's Magazine has a strong community of illustrators who encourage each other and collaborate together as a result of meeting in the virtual world. Each profile reveals a more in-depth view of their practice, and you can find them online through the links at the back of book.

I have long been fascinated with fashion: I studied Printed Textiles for Fashion at Brighton University and I continue to attend fashion shows and to profile fashion designers. The way in which we choose to dress is the best outward manifestation of our lives and personalities, so clothing is and will continue to be, one of the most defining aspects of humankind. As a creative medium of expression fashion cannot be bettered, and like many others I adore the imaginative designs of the best fashion designers and stylists.

Yet I've always had a conflicted relationship with fashion, constantly worrying over how our obsession affects not only the makers and the environment but also the psyche of the wearers who constantly demand new and better clothes. In the past we were bound to the fabrics and garments that could be sourced and made locally, but nowadays the wholesale divorce from strong societal mores has met our ever greater capabilities to create wondrous garments. Where once people treasured a few important items that were lovingly mended and passed down over the years, the global capitalist system has made us accustomed to the easy acquisition of ever cheaper fast fashion that willingly feeds our insatiable appetite for self-expression. Instead of carefully mending treasured garments we can purchase mountains of fabulous clothes at the mere click of a button, ironically replacing the time saved from making and mending with... shopping.

My first book, Amelia's Anthology of Illustration, asked illustrators to explore little-known renewable technologies to prevent catastrophic climate change. For this book I asked illustrators to represent the best in ethical fashion design. Forget the sackcloth designs of yesteryear, the new breed of ethical designers can now stand alone alongside the best of mainstream fashion design. They quite rightly think of themselves as designers first and foremost, ethical makers next. A commitment to ethical practice requires an active engagement with all levels of the design and manufacturing process, but rather than this inhibiting their practice, many designers find delight in (often self-imposed) ethical restrictions which force them to find new methods of working.

The designers that appear in this book work in a range of different ways, from the use of carefully sourced recycled, organic, local and/or fairtrade materials to a thoughtful purpose behind the entire supply chain. I call this ethical fashion design, for truly sustainable fashion has ethics at the heart of it - where care of people and the planet are considered a priority. In the UK there is considerable support for ethical fashion - many designers show their collections at the Estethica eco fashion exhibition during London Fashion Week and are given guidance by organisations such as the Ethical Fashion Forum and the Centre for Sustainable Fashion. Those with most experience now campaign and teach their skills to others as the benefits of acting sustainably become ever more apparent. The interviews with ethical fashion designers reveal the profound thought and effort that has gone into their practices.

Illustration has a unique ability to add an extra layer of creative interpretation that can render a product more attractive to potential customers. Ethical designers often work within an extremely tight budget and need all the help they can get to create a strong and desirable brand. My wish is that this book will inspire many useful and helpful collaborations, some of which have already happened as a result of illustrators contacting designers when they set out to complete my open brief.

More than anything, an ethical approach to fashion needs to become mainstream practice, and for this to happen it needs to be judged both on aesthetics and functionality against the best that other designers can produce. To avoid the ghettoisation of ethical designers, Amelia's Magazine covers ethical practitioners next to great independently produced design, and this book is no different. Many of the images herein have already accompanied articles on our web pages, proving that illustration is the perfect way to get images across in an inspiring manner. This is especially true during periods of quick turnaround where photography just cannot compete - a practice we put into good effect during London Fashion Week. Unlike fashion photography, illustration does not require a big team to create something unique: just a starting image or idea and the hand of a lone creative. Perhaps, as we head towards an age of austerity, this is one of the reasons why fashion illustration is currently enjoying one of its cyclical renaissances.

This book is a clarion call to listen to and support all those who inspire change in this world. To illustrators who help promote ideas and products in oh-so-appealing ways, and to everyone who has a hand in the way that we produce and consume fashion. Beauty rapidly turns ugly when it is not founded in ethical practice, and my sincerest hope is that in a few years this book will be outmoded because it has become standard practice to consider all the implications of how a garment is made.

Read on and be inspired...

The world of design is constantly evolving so please do catch up with me online at Amelia's Magazine, where you can contribute illustrations and read about the most exciting new creative endeavours on a daily basis. And don't forget to check out my Skype interviews with the talented illustrators that I profile within these pages.

www.ameliasmagazine.com
twitter.com/ameliasmagazine
www.facebook.com/amelias.mag
Skype interviews: www.youtube.com/user/ameliashouse

Contents

Fashion Illustrators

Ethical Fashion Designers

When did your interest in fashion illustration begin?

I think it really took off when I started my illustration degree. I was already interested in portraiture so when I started to research other illustrators I realised how fabulous fashion illustration can be and the transition worked perfectly. I love the fantastic colours, shapes, styles and textures that are possible when describing fashion.

What styles or eras of art inspire you the most?

I love 1920's fashion illustrations, and the exquisiteness of the Art Deco style. As well as these, I'm inspired by Japanese illustrations, especially detailed woodblock prints depicting women. David Downtown has been a big inspiration too.

How do you create your fashion illustrations?

I've become really confident in drawing straight onto my Mac with my trusty Wacom tablet. I start with a simple line drawing and build up the layers and detail as I go. I love getting to the stage when I can bring in scanned textures to experiment with the way an image looks.

What does your workspace look like?

I share a flat with my boyfriend and I work on a lovely wooden table in the corner of our living room; surrounded by my books, computer and favourite tools. A homely feeling makes me creative so it's very cosy.

How does being in Yorkshire influence the way that you design?

Yorkshire is great. There is so much tranquillity and elegance here, and the beautiful colours, line, shapes and textures of nature have inspired the way I work.

Why do you have an obsession with cats and birds?

As a child, we always had at least three cats in the house and I would dress them up in baby clothes. I drew cats all the time and I still draw cats when I'm sitting in front of the telly... they're so relaxing. My love of birds is down to my Dad, who taught us the wood pigeon's song. It became very special to us because we'd make him do impressions. After he died, my Mum and I began crafting old clothes into brooches, cards and bags and we used birds as a theme in memory of him. We collected different pieces of bird art and hung them up as inspiration.

What exciting things have happened as a result of social networking?

I really didn't expect to get as much out of social networking as I have: it's given me the opportunity to be involved in group projects, hear about competitions and find illustration jobs. As a result I've worked for online magazines that have given me some great promotion and I've formed some great relationships with other illustrators, especially through working for Amelia's Magazine. I have just helped to set up the Tea and Crayons illustration collective consisting of six regular contributors to Amelia's Magazine and we aim to support each other and hold collaborative exhibitions.

Since illustrating Ada Zanditon you seem to have struck up a good online friendship. Why do you think she likes your work so much?

self-portrait

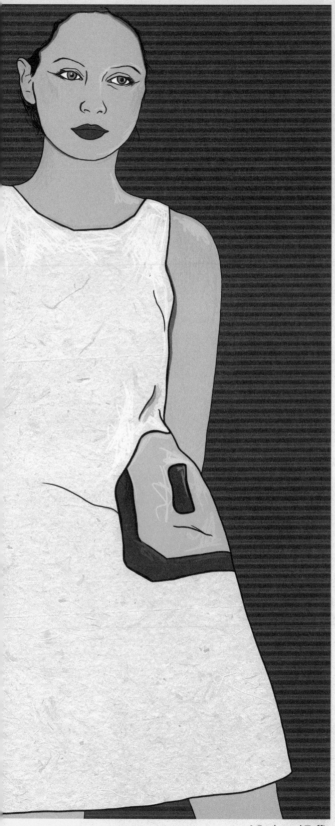

Her work is so bold and sculptural, yet classically beautiful, I loved it from the moment I saw her collections. I work with bold colours and textures in my illustrations to make sure the clothes are the main focus, similar to the way that she creates her own illustrations, so perhaps she appreciates the way I work.

Why is ethical fashion so important to you?
I think my interest in ethical fashion design comes from reworking scrap materials with my mum when I was a child - I love the idea of recycling materials to make something new and beautiful. I collect bits of material and paper to use in my work, and I think it's great that designers do this on a bigger scale; if it's possible to be an ethical designer, why would you not be? I plan to produce ethical fashion illustrations with an editorial twist for my final degree year.

What do you hope to do in the future?
I would, of course, love a career in fashion illustration. My ultimate dream is to work as a freelance illustrator from my own inspiring studio, overlooking a beautiful garden.

^ Foale and Tuffin
Roksanda Ilincic S/S 2011 >

Ada Zanditon S/S 2011
The Pyramora

Ada Zanditon

Ada Zanditon necklace from S/S 2010, The Colony

Ada Zanditon was inspired to use ethically and environmentally conscious solutions in fashion design after she heard a talk given by Katharine Hamnett. **Katharine speaks from a very authentic and informed position that inspired me to question the purpose of design and how it can impact the planet.** For both ecological and economic reasons Ada decided to focus on design processes that eliminate waste. In practical terms she creates zero waste patterns and saves any remnants to use in other garments or as stuffing or binding. **It's a matter of innovation and efficient resource management.** She is also careful about where she sources her fabrics, finding it more of a help than a hindrance to have ecological constraints over what she can choose.

Her clothes are known for their sculptural qualities, a fact she attributes to her fascination with sculptures, architecture and geometry from an early age. She is particularly attracted to biomimicry in design and is inspired by the work of artist Anish Kapoor. **But what I most like is the intimate connection between clothing and the human form. It is the presence of the human figure that brings a design to life.**

Each season Ada creates print designs from a combination of digital photographs, images taken on a Lomographic Coloursplash film camera and illustrations in pencil, ink and watercolour. The different elements are scanned into Photoshop and Illustrator and provide the core concept for the ensuing collection. For example, corals photographed at London Zoo, paintings of the Sahara Desert and ink drawings of the Great Pyramid formed the basis of her most recent collection. Digital prints on organic silk and cotton fabrics are an essential part of each collection.

Viktoria Modesta has been a muse since the start of her musical career, and they work together to create her stage outfits. **My made to measure couture outfits are based on my signature concepts but the individual performer is very much at the heart of the creation.** Becky Jones of Saint Saviour also got in touch and together they collaborated with lighting designer Jeffrey Michael Baker to enhance her costume with tube lighting.

Fellow designer Luca Romanyi has created bespoke jewellery for three of Ada's collections. For S/S 2010 The Colony shredded end-of-line bank notes were suspended within honeycomb structures that mimic the chemical structure of recycled polycarbonate. The pieces for her A/W 2010 Echolocation collection were created using 3form's Ecoresin, which has incredible reflective qualities. For S/S 2011's The Pyramora the pair collaborated with Johnson Tiles' Material Lab, printing bespoke designs onto durable tiling from their Prismatics recycled ceramic range, combining triangular sections (a good shape for zero waste) with vegetable tanned leather and Swarovski crystals.

Sustainability has to be economically desirable and sustainable fashion has to be the most sexy, cutting edge, interesting, intriguing way of dressing. Such is the reality of human behaviour. She is currently most excited about the 360 degree vision approach to sustainability, which uses ethical solutions wherever possible based on each design. **There has been a rapid increase in interest around eco design so it will be interesting to watch how advances in innovation unfold over the next few years.**

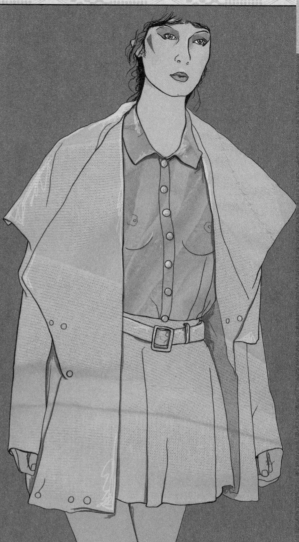

Ada Zanditon S/S 2011, The Pyramora

Fifi Bijoux rutile quartz jewellery

You were one of the first jewellery designers to take an ethical stance on manufacturing of high end jewellery in the UK. What have you achieved?

I set up the British Ethical Jewellery Association to create a set of auditable ethical standards for the industry. This has since been superseded by the ethics working committee of the National Association of Goldsmiths which has adopted the same aims, helping to enable relationships between jewellers and small-scale mining projects. NAG has nearly a thousand members, so it is the perfect platform to achieve our aim of supporting jewellers in the UK to lead the way in adopting ethical sourcing as a core business value. In the UK there is a real will to embrace better ethical practices and a fairtraded logo for jewellery will be agreed on shortly.

Have you seen much change in the industry since you started Fifi Bijoux?

The most remarkable change has come from gem and diamond-producing countries such as Tanzania, Madagascar and Namibia, who are now cutting and polishing the gems before export. This represents a huge shift in technical skills and economics since a large percentage of a gem's value is added at this stage. The lapidary art of stone cutting requires a high degree of technical and scientific expertise in order to create the sophisticated facets expected by western customers, and this can be provided by modern lasers. Gravity mining provides a relatively low impact solution for gold extraction. It is really important that producers in developing countries are able to access markets and this is where organisations such as the Fairtrade Foundation and membership bodies like NAG can create quantum shifts; an individual jeweller may struggle with the process of sourcing gold, exporting it from a developing country, refining it and processing it into a usable material to create jewellery. However, by acting collectively with support resources in place, this becomes considerably less daunting.

Do you think there is hope for change in the mining community, following the Chilean mining disaster?

I think this is a perfect opportunity to drive improvements in the South American mines. The Chilean mining disaster commanded an international audience, giving the issue a whole new place in peoples' hearts. Health and safety standards have been incredibly slack in the past, with the value of life being all too little. Some mines will require huge investment to make them compliant with best practice, with even the most basic safety measures absent in many small mines. Providing helmets, dust masks, reliable lighting, proper oxygen supplies, winches and an escape plan would be a good start.

What ethical practices have you seen adopted by big brands?

Cartier has committed to source from the small family-owned Eurocantera mine in Honduras that operates to exceptionally high standards of social and environmental stewardship. Wal-Mart has created the Love, Earth brand which is noteworthy because it is the first big company to use completely traceable gold and silver. Their environmental criteria may not be as rigorous as many would like, but they should be credited with promoting transparency of the supply chain. Michael J. Kowalski (CEO of Tiffany) has been one of the most powerful voices in influencing policy, having committed considerable resources towards mining reform.

Do you have any plans to make more large show pieces?

A few years ago we launched a collection of limited edition pieces made out of rutile quartz mined in Bahia, Brazil. Only a few of each design were produced since the mine is due to close shortly, and all the profits from the gem cutting are invested back into organic farming in the local area. I plan to design some new cuts before the mine closes down, and I'm also working on some dramatic cocktail ring designs using pearls, rubies, sapphires and fancy cut diamonds.

What one piece of expensive jewellery can a woman not live without?

Perhaps it's because I tend to use my hands when I talk but I think I would have to say an exquisite statement ring. Hands are often used to attract the line of vision to your best feature and, best of all, you can see a ring yourself whereas you can't always see your own earrings or pendant. I often focus on my diamond ring when I am thinking, finding myself lost in the light fractions of the diamond.

Natsuki Otani

FASHION ILLUSTRATOR

self-portrait

Illustrator and blog keeper Natsuki Otani has a huge online presence which supports not only herself but a host of other young creatives. It can be tough sometimes, and her Illustration Rally blog often keeps her up late at night, but she keeps a firm grasp on what next needs updating so that she has time to rest at the weekends.

Illustration Rally was started after Natsuki first graduated and found it hard to keep illustrating without a project to work on. What started as a bit of self-promotion soon opened up to everyone so she could keep up the pace. **The basic rally format takes a theme that can easily be broken down into single illustrations, like the alphabet, months of the year and European countries.** She posts the illustrations as they come in, and she was surprised by how quickly it has become popular as illustra-

tors looking for new briefs chanced upon it. Now she also runs artist features, reviews and event listings.

Natsuki likes the way that publications such as Amelia's Magazine make an effort to engage with the illustration community on social networking sites, and she discovered just how powerful Twitter is when she was featured in Computer Arts magazine simply on the recommendation of a friend on Twitter. She's quite shy in person but finds she can be much more confident in approaching people, especially potential clients, when she is online. She currently lives in Cambridge so the internet is also a powerful and necessary way to communicate with the outside world.

Natsuki recommends that all burgeoning illustrators should get online. **Try everything until you find the most comfortable place to hang out, be it on a blog, Twitter, Facebook or Tumblr.** She thinks it is much easier to maintain multiple social networks once you are used to them. **Start talking to other creatives and follow what they do, be polite and helpful, and they will be, in return. It's possible to be much braver online.** She is very proud of the friendly community she has built up on Illustration Rally.

A surreal, psychedelic flavour permeates Natsuki's colourful drawings, despite the fact that she favours black for her own clothes. In similarly contradictory fashion she likes to draw people drinking and smoking, even though she does neither herself. Thanks to her traditional Japanese training she prefers to draw her subjects in a realistic manner, but she is also hugely influenced by Japanese Manga comic art. She comments that whilst music tastes are usually the defining feature of teenage friendships in the UK, fashion reigns supreme in Japan. She draws straight onto paper with inks and pens, then scans the finished image into the computer. Ethical designs appeal particularly to her because they have a stronger concept and meaning to work with.

Natsuki lived in Tokyo before coming to study in England, taking a degree in Illustration at Norwich University College of the Arts. She likes cooking for herself, walking and watching how the seasons change. She believes that finding happiness is an important step towards leading a more sustainable existence.

Lu Flux A/W 2009, Old Believer

Lu Flux S/S 2010, Eco Life of Riley

Nina
Dolcetti

ETHICAL SHOE DESIGNER:
ELISALEX GRUNFELD DE CASTRO

Were you already considering how to make ethical shoes whilst you were studying at Cordwainers?

Absolutely. I come from a family of ethical fashion pioneers (Orsola de Castro of From Somewhere is my Mum), so it was a no-brainer for me. I know too much about the quantity of waste produced by the fashion industry and the exploitation of people and environment, so of course I was set on running my label as ethically and morally as I could.

When did you first start to work with your signature wedge and what was the process of finding the perfect shape?

The first drawing I did of my signature curved wedge was in a quiet moment at my first Esthetica exhibition at London Fashion Week in 2008, when I was eight months pregnant. The wave of inspiration for my next collection had just hit me and I was absorbed in my new designs. It wasn't until much later that I realised that the curve of the wedge was the exact line, only reversed, of the instep. And thinking about it now, I think the pregnancy definitely had something to do with it too!

Where do you source your materials from?

I source my offcuts from anywhere and everywhere. I've found amazing textured leathers in markets in Spain, been given boxes of beautiful offcuts from other designers, and raided bins in factories. I can find a use for even the smallest scraps. The vegetable tanned leather comes from Italy, and the heels and platforms in cork and wood are hand turned in Norfolk.

Why is the chrome tanning process so poisonous?

The process of tanning leather with chromium is incredibly harmful for the people who work in the industry. They will experience ulcers, chronic dermatitis and severe respiratory illnesses if they breathe in the fumes or the chemicals come into direct contact with their skin. The chromium-laden waste from tanneries is dumped in landfills and it is extremely polluting to the environment.

How did your relationship with a small family factory in east London come about?

I had just moved back to London from Spain, and was putting my first collection together. Up until then I had been making all my shoes by myself, but with my new, more ambitious designs I knew I didn't have enough experience or time to produce entire collections single-handedly. Time was running out and I was freaking out... then I spoke to the people who make my lasts and they gave me the number of the factory. It turns out they are probably the most established and respected factory in the UK, very

conveniently a short drive from my studio - so I've been with them ever since.

How does the mentorship program with Estethica work?

The mentorship program with Estethica was a huge boost for me. It involved a number of one-to-one sessions where we discussed everything from costs to inspiration and it couldn't have come at a better time. Bouncing ideas around with someone experienced allowed me to really tap into what inspires me and after the hard schlep of the recession it helped me to re-focus and re-motivate myself. I think my best collections so far have come as a result of the mentoring.

Nina Dolcetti S/S 2011

Where will you be in ten years time?

In ten years time I like to think that my label will be going much the same as it is now... just a lot more smoothly. I aim to expand the Nina Dolcetti team and start a shop facility on my website, but I still want to retain the underground cult reputation that I have now.

Holly Fulton S/S 2011

Ada Zanditon S/S 2011

Paul Costelloe S/S 2011

Paul Costelloe S/S 2011

Animal Bandido A/W 2010

Prophetik

ETHICAL FASHION DESIGNER: JEFF GARNER

Where did you learn to design?

From growing up in the woods of Tennessee and watching nature. The synergy of God's design in nature is the wisest teacher. For technical design I went the route of mentors and hands-on hard work versus design school.

How does doing business in Franklin, Tennessee, compare to working in London? And how has it affected the way you design?

I believe everyone is connected to where they were born and raised, therefore creating art out of passion at my home farm is a beautiful energy. The air still smells the same, like nowhere else. I believe it gives me a solid place to design from, like the roots of the mango trees that hold the shorelines together to protect against a hurricane. London allows the designs to breathe; it is a catalyst for change in fashion, supporting the sustainable design practices of the future. And in both places I have a horse to ride - to keep nature close by.

Where did you show before you came here? And how does it compare to being in the UK during London Fashion Week?

I have shown in most major marketplaces: Las Vegas, Los Angeles, Paris, New York, Milan, Atlanta, Vancouver. All are very different from London. I was asked to show in London when the Estethica team discovered our line in the States, and of course I said yes. I felt as if I had come home as soon as I arrived - the family-type energy of Estethica is amazing. It is why I decided to show in London, and in what I would call its sister city, Vancouver. The UK really supports designers, especially in sustainable fashion, which is missing in other markets. I feel that in the UK everyone supports each other in their art and passion, versus being competitive in nature.

How do you reconcile flying across the world several times a year with producing a collection ethically?

I physically have to be places in order to create motion in our movement for sustainability. I have not eaten fast food or non-local food since I was a teen and I live and work simply. I drive a Prius, a motorbike or ride a horse in Tennessee. I fly within the US on stand-by, taking a seat on the flight that has not been occupied, thereby not directly supporting the need to fly. Sort of like the carpooling idea. I never fly for vacation but only to serve with my non-profit educational program Appleseed Expeditions or for fashion weeks or shows.

What does being ethical mean to you?

It means living a life that serves a purpose other than oneself. Walking in the manner of what one knows is right and good, consuming less, having honour and integrity in business no matter what the selfish gain or loss may be. True character is shown when no one is looking. Being ethical in fashion means sourcing fabrics that will last and have the lowest impact when they are being made - whether recycled, sustainable, or repurposed, using dyes that do not leave our water systems with toxic waste nor harm our lungs and affect our breathing. It also means being honest with retailers and consumers.

How do you pass this on to your fashion students?

I inspire them to think outside of our current cycles of design and production - to challenge that conformity with better ways to work in terms of using less energy and fewer harmful chemical processes.

How did you set up the factory in Tennessee?

Many years of trying, and being stubborn. I had a vision and with much time and effort, the pieces all came together.

Why the Fleur de Lis logo? What does this represent?

Without sounding like a history teacher, the Fleur de Lis gained its symbolic position when a young English king was going to fight a decisive battle. Along the way he prayed that he should win the battle honourably for all, and then he saw the lily in the field. He won the battle that day and made the Fleur de Lis the heraldic symbol on his shield of armour. Another leader, Joan of Arc, flew her flag with the Fleur de Lis symbol as well, again representing that she was chosen but not alone in her quest and calling for a higher purpose.

How does one look after individualism and yet work harmoniously for the greater collective good?

That question has really been unanswered in my life. It is a journey and process and I believe everyone should focus on the calling in their life for the greater collective good and not worry about the self. There are lots of wolves that feed off the free-thinking and giving artist, but I don't believe it should change us. I cannot protect my designs because as soon as they have hit the runways they are alive all over the world for anyone to copy, which they do; many have no conscience when it comes to business. But I think it all comes back around and artists should continue loving and creating. One day the business minds that capitalise off our creativity and inspiration will help us, instead of taking advantage of us for their own personal gain. Such selfishness cannot last and one day we will all have to answer for our own actions despite what is popular and accepted in our modern day culture.

You use hemp - why is it a good material?

Hemp is three times stronger than cotton because it is the longest fibre, hence its strength. It holds its shape above all other natural fibres, does not fade, is UV-resistant and anti-microbial along with being resistant to mildew and mould. It is great for travel or outside wardrobes. Hemp takes natural dyes almost ten times more than cotton because of its porous nature and it softens naturally without fibre degradation. It is breathable, so can be used for all seasons. Where growth is concerned, it does not require pesticides or herbicides and harvests in 120 days without extracting the ground of nutrients, so other succeeding crops can be planted. Even the deeper roots of hemp help protect from runoff, preserving topsoil which is enriched with organic matter by the shedding of hemp leaves. Hemp produces more fibre yield per acre than any other source I know of, roughly 250% more than cotton fibre.

Why are natural dyes better than synthetic ones?

Natural dyes are better for skin, which is porous, and waste from natural dye is without question better for our water systems, soil and plant life. Some amazing one-of-a-kind colours can be created through aged garden-grown indigo or marigold.

What prompted the collaboration with Nina Dolcetti and what was the process of design for the shoes?

I had a vision of working with her so I emailed her and she said yes. Then she came to Tennessee - I took her to Elvis's home in Memphis, two-stepping in Nashville, horse riding - and it was a done deal, Tennessee-style. The inspiration was created and I believe we both became muses in each other's designs for the season.

If you design the menswear for yourself, then who do you design the womenswear for? Who is the ideal woman to wear it?

She is a romantic creature frolicking in the same woods that she has stepped foot in since she was a young girl, where she dreams of a future adventurer who will one day stumble upon her as she is picking flowers. And he in turn has travelled the world for a dream that he eventually finds in her. Then he realises what he has been looking for... and a new adventure begins where the ideal meets reality.

How did your collaboration with Griffin come about?

I was writing poetry in a wine bar in Tennessee when a young gentleman approached my table to ask if I was the designer of Prophetik. He looked like a similar poetic soul and he wanted to know if I would be interested in designing something soulful for Griffin Technology; the sustainable results have a beautiful connection to the consumer that stands out in a world full of throwaway electronics.

You have some very high profile friends - how so?

I don't think we pick our friends - they just cross our paths at certain times in our life for a purpose and it is our job to listen to that purpose. I have found myself in the most random situations and "high profile" interactions, but we are all beautiful souls waiting to be discovered by another. One should always stay true to self no matter what the environment yields.

Tell us the story of the riding boots that you have been wearing for 17 years...

Well, my Western riding boots are even older since they were passed down by my father. Of course a good leather boot can last a very long time with a new sole. I believe in using things for that which they were designed for, so I still ride in my old boots most days. If this world crashes and we head back to the old times I will be well-prepared. At one time a village economy was all we ever needed. Then we were introduced to more and thus we craved more; commerce and money were created. Today's society must grow, consume and produce more in order to make the economy go round, yet we face economic crises.

What, in your eyes, is needed to create a garment that will last a lifetime?

Strong fibre like hemp or recycled or repurposed leather. It needs a great cut and if it needs buttons or zippers, they have to be the best. Great sewing has to be incorporated with maybe a waxed thread or poly/hemp thread to keep strength. I have my great grandmother's side saddle with a red velour seat, which has lasted over four generations. I believe it can be done. In the old days a person was known by the waistcoat or coat which they wore because it was well made to last. Those garments were part of the character of a person, yet nowadays fast trends and cheap manufacturing create clothing that does not last, feeding the cycle of consumerism. No wonder most are seeking their identity. Fashion teaches them to be a rock star one season and a bohemian hippie the next season. They are not the character inside, only an image that will never reveal the true self of an individual.

Declare yourself and you shall find a lifetime of joy.

Lu FLux A/W 2010
Dame & Knight

Graham Coxon

Paul Costelloe S/S 2011

self-portrait

Bex Glover

Illustrator and graphic designer Bex Glover works under the moniker of Severn Studios in Bristol, where she moved after being made redundant from her job in London. Fortunately this was the kickstart she needed to go freelance after seven years of professional employment as a graphic designer, and it seemed a good time to pursue her love of illustration. She sometimes misses London but of course nowadays it's possible to be remotely available wherever you are based, so on balance she feels it was a good move to head back to where she grew up. Although freelance life has its ups, downs and uncertainties "I like being my own boss in charge of my future," she says. "It's scary but exciting."

Her graphic design background has given Bex a solid grounding in the use of computer design applications and lots of good experience in dealing with clients, account handling and how illustration works commercially in advertising and editorial. When Bex discovered Amelia's Magazine via Twitter she thought it might be a good promotional platform so she began to volunteer her fashion illustrations. "I especially like illustrating high-end catwalk looks because they are so expressive." Twitter has enabled her to get in touch with loads of fellow illustrators, whose advice, tips and inspiration have been invaluable. "I've really had to concentrate on getting my work out there and getting my name known - which my website, blog and social networking have been absolutely invaluable in doing."

Since her first artistic dabbles on the walls of her childhood home in a West Country village, Bex has been inspired to paint. Combining hand-rendered and digital techniques she draws figures by hand with inks, acrylics and markers, then creates watercolour and spray effects to scan and combine with digital textures and colours in Photoshop. For an 'urban meets ornate' twist she adds flourishes and embellishments. "I'm influenced by graffiti and street art so I like the contrast between flat solid colours, rough paint marks and sharp edges against delicate, detailed textures."

Whilst working she listens to everything from hip-hop, soul, dub and Brazilian to reggae, jazz and garage. "The type of music affects my work but there's no particular formula." Some days she listens to plays on the radio. Bristol is particularly known for its vibrant street culture and she has recently been involved with some great magazines and collaborative group exhibitions, including the Temwa, Art for Africa exhibition which showcased some of the best new urban artists and designers.

Howies was her ethical clothing brand of choice because she likes their whole mantra of good quality, low impact clothing. "There's a good vibe about the business, which seems really down to earth."

Her ambition now is to get more editorial illustration work for magazines, books and for fashion retail. "I love nice packaging, displays and interiors, so it would be amazing to one day see my art in the windows of somewhere like Harvey Nics." Currently working from a spare room in her house, she hopes soon to move into a shared studio surrounded by other artists by whom she will feel inspired. "Ultimately I want to be happy, healthy and making money from doing what I love."

Howies S/S 2010

Howies

ETHICAL FASHION DESIGN

Howies has since 1995 pioneered the creation of ethical active clothing with a strong design aesthetic. Based in Cardigan Bay, Wales, the company has built up a devoted fan base via its affiliation with outdoor sports such as surfing, mountain biking and skateboarding. Products are made from high performing sustainable fabrics that will last, with a proportion of profits ploughed back into grass-roots social and environmental projects via the Earth Tax. Although some clothes are made in China and Turkey they ensure best practice by employing the same factories as other companies they trust, such as M&S.

The founders of Howies, former ad execs Claire and David Hieatt, recently departed the company in order to concentrate on other ventures, which has left designer Pete Davies in the position of brand guardian. Howies is currently owned by American clothing giant Timberland, but their ethical foundations are such an integral part of the brand's ethos that nothing looks likely to shift them. However, some aspects of production are destined for change, including the way their much-loved catalogue is produced. More money will be spent on the website, which will not only reduce the carbon footprint of all that shipping, but also allow Howies to reach a far bigger potential market.

Charlie Le Mindu A/W 2010

Romeo Pires S/S 2011

Ivana Basilotta

Ivana Basilotta is Italian but has lived in Germany as well as the UK. She channels her observations of different cultures into her work, sometimes the ideas flowing so fast that her pen can't keep up and her scissors can't cut the fabric fast enough. Quite often she only realises she was inspired by a certain idea once the collection has been finished. Having previously studied business Ivana is well placed to run her label, and feels that a good business knowledge is as important as the creative force of a design house.

A committed vegetarian, she designs with peace silk, which is made in India without the killing of the silk moth. Because peace silk is spun as a fibre rather than reeled as a thread it is warmer and softer than ordinary silk. "I cannot imagine eating meat," she says. "I find it strange that people eat dead animals." She feels that being a vegetarian brings a great sense of freedom and well being, and it is an easy way to lead a greener life. "Farm land that could directly produce food for humans is used to farm and feed animals for slaughter, which uses up far more resources." She does not like to imagine the stress and sorrow that farmed animals must experience, and wants no part in it.

Her biodegradable fabrics are sourced from certified producers. Modal is a super soft, light, silky fabric that is made of 100% cellulose extracted from sustainable farmed beech trees. It has a similar texture to silk, is cool to the touch and very absorbent. Bemberg is another cellulose fibre fabric that has a luxurious drape and provides a graceful, flowing silhouette. Ivana's collections are made in India because of the fine craftsmanship, but she also sources some eco fabrics from Turkey.

Despite only starting the label in 2009 she is already selling worldwide due to some excellent sales agents who believe in the label and her skills. She uses creative visualisation to keep her goals in the foremost of her mind. "I always wish to work with people who are good at what they do and keen to work with me... and in one way or another they appear in my life."

To maintain the beauty of the natural world she recommends that we start with ourselves by adopting spiritual values that will change the wider world. "As our thought vibrations change the levels of happiness will increase, and our actions will automatically be of greater benefit. We are powerful when we realise we have choices."

J.Maskrey A/W 2010

Imogen Belfield A/W 2010

Charlie Le Mindu A/W 2010

J.Maskrey A/W 2010

Katie Harnett

FASHION ILLUSTRATOR

Why does your style of illustration fit so well with clothes made by Tara Starlet and why did you decide to take inspiration from 50's pin up posters?

I chose to illustrate garments from Tara Starlet partly because I love their clothes, but also because it gave me the chance to try something exciting with my illustrations. I have always loved 50's pin up posters, and from Tara Starlet's website it was clear that this was an influence of theirs too, so it seemed a perfect opportunity to use some of the styling and poses from that era for my illustrations. I think my method of working fits with the Tara Starlet ethos as well - a combination of old and new.

How do you construct your illustrations and what inspires you?

I draw out and map the image in pencil, then paint a watercolour wash, then colour in some more on Photoshop. I tend to work in overly time-consuming ways so I can experiment and see what comes out best. I love the work of children's illustrator Meg Hunt, and she uses a lot of pattern so I try to do the same in my own work. Although there is quite a wide gap between children's illustration and high fashion I think there are links, and I like doing both. I always look at the clothes worn by the characters in a story because they give important clues to personality.

Why is it important that ethical fashion designers make desirable clothes?

I think it's vitally important that ethical companies provide desirable clothes, firstly so that ethical fashion isn't seen as a fad or a compromise but is able to compete directly with other clothes on the market and secondly because being ethical shouldn't be the selling point of a company, but rather should be a given - all clothing companies should produce great clothes which are also ethically sourced.

self-portrait

Ramón Gurillo A/W 2010

Cooperative Designs A/W 2010

Ann-Sofie Back A/W 2010

Cooperative Designs A/W 2010

Ramón Gurillo A/W 2010

You are constantly experimenting - what have been your most successful experiments in illustration so far?

It's very hard to pick a most successful experiment, although there have certainly been a lot which have gone horribly wrong! I'm currently experimenting a lot with working digitally and I think my most successful outcomes are where I pair this way of working with my more traditional drawing and painting skills.

Why did you set yourself an aim to appear in Amelia's Magazine when you started college and in what way has it been helpful to work for the online magazine?

I was a devotee of the print magazines, and set myself the target of entering an open brief and hopefully being published in the magazine (I'm a big fan of setting targets, both realistic and hopelessly unachievable). I was really disappointed when I heard there would be no more print issues of the magazine, and so when I got the opportunity to work for the website it was very exciting. Illustrating for the website has been great for expanding my portfolio and promoting my work. It also allows me to experiment with different styles and techniques and get quick feedback from people, which I hugely appreciate.

How is your fashion themed range of greetings cards and prints getting along?

Working for Amelia's Magazine online has shown me how much I love fashion illustration, and so making fashion-themed cards seems like a natural transition. I'm starting with a small range of five, but I think it will be a rolling project as I enjoy it so much, and I will hopefully bring out new cards to reflect changing styles and seasons.

Can you tell us more about your latest collaborative children's book?

I recently went to the Swedish Arctic and I found it so inspiring, from the scenery to the folklore to the architecture, that I decided to set a children's book there. The book is titled The Light Which Can Be Heard, after the Sami people's name for the Northern Lights, and it will follow a little girl's magical journey. I have been writing and drawing together with a friend since we were in primary school, so we are collaborating on this children's book, which is still in its early stages but will hopefully do justice to our many years of working together. I have also just started planning out another book about letters (I love getting letters) so I have plenty to be getting on with.

How has being from Sheffield and now based in Bristol affected the way you work?

Although I have been surrounded by urban landscapes I have always been inspired by nature; I wanted to grow up to be David Attenborough (a forlorn hope). I think that landscapes do affect work to a certain extent, but I haven't been tempted to illustrate very urban scenes yet, perhaps because my art is more about escapism. Both Bristol and Sheffield are fairly busy cities but are not too far away from lovely scenery, so they suit me perfectly.

Why has social networking opened up possibilities to engage with companies and clients?

I think social networking has made a huge difference to how freelancers work, allowing illustrators to create and develop professional opportunities which would have been very difficult to achieve otherwise. Social networking allows direct contact with clients and companies who are difficult to get in contact with in the 'real world'. By creating relationships online you come into contact with a huge range of like-minded people that you might never have met otherwise. Especially for someone like me who often works from home, social networking gives a wide source of inspiration, feedback and constructive criticism, which is invaluable, and is also sometimes a welcome distraction from work.

What are your plans for the next five years?

In the next five years I hope to do a lot: complete my existing children's books and start more, find new projects and collaborations to occupy me and discover yet more exciting and inspiring things to do. I love all types of illustration, and really want to experiment with as many different things as I can. I also have a vague plan to move to London if I can afford it.

Lastly, why the moniker teabelle?

The name 'teabelle' comes from my little white poodle Belle, who shared my love of drinking tea.

Basso & Brooke A/W 2010

How did the idea of working with old porcelain come about?

I was tired of producing other peoples' ideas (as a stage producer) so in 2007 I decided to start working on my own project, which soon developed into my rapidly growing label, Sägen. I go to flea markets as often as I can for inspiration and to collect source material; I have amassed a huge collection of vintage buttons as well as piles of chipped and damaged porcelain that is no longer wanted. I like to work with my hands and I love turning items from the past into modern accessories.

Sägen means Old Saga in Swedish - why did you chose this name for your brand?

I come from a small island called Gotland in the middle of the Baltic Sea and I have wonderful memories of listening to all the old myths when I was a kid. I came up with the idea for Sägen when I was there and the name reflects my interest in recycling a little bit of history into new treasures, so I find the name very suitable.

How do you cut the porcelain and set it in silver?

I cut and grind the porcelain with machines, which is a very dirty, dusty and dangerous job: I have been close to losing my fingers many times. When I am working in my basement studio I forget about everything else, instead focusing on the patterns that I am obsessed with. I decide what shapes to make up depending on the motifs in the porcelain, then I set the porcelain in silver (which is 98% recycled) so that it curves, bends and stretches around the shape I have cut out.

How do you decide what to do with the different patterns?

I catalogue my porcelain regularly so that it is easier to decide what patterns will make up the next collection. There are so many inspiring patterns to work with that I will never run out of ideas. My most recent collection is called Dining with Grandma. The Swedish Classics line uses our most famous Swedish graphic design patterns from the 1950's and 60's, seen by some as the golden age of porcelain design. Dutchess Garden is more bohemian and makes use of turn of the century designs that feature lots of roses and bird patterns. I am deeply in love with kitsch

motifs as well as the factory stamps that are often very beautiful in themselves.

How do people react to these classic porcelain patterns?

For people in Scandinavia the jewellery designs will evoke many memories. Some of the motifs remind me of Sunday dinners at my Grandmother's house, hence the name Dining with Grandma. People usually stand for a long time looking at the pieces, than they start to remember and recognise where they have seen these patterns on plates and cups a long time ago. Sometimes they get sentimental... or they laugh. I love sharing stories about the designs: how old they are, their names, where they come from and what I like about them.

Can you tell us anything about the most famous designs?

Scandinavian retro porcelain has become very popular again and some of the most popular patterns are being reproduced. Stig Lindberg is the most famous designer of the modern period, and his porcelain designs Spisa Ribb, Berså and Terma were used in many thousands of homes. Today, his work is highly coveted, and even simple pieces can generate high prices. I give people the opportunity to wear designs from this golden period next to their skin, close to their hearts.

What has happened since you visited Estethica in London?

The response has been great: I have sold to many new shops around the world including Isetan in Japan, and I have been invited to Brazil with Lu Flux, which is exciting because I love her designs.

How do you juggle the demands of running a small business with having a small child?

I work hard but I like the variety and I get a kick out of deciding how to run this business on my own. I am also very passionate about everything and I love a lot - it helps that I have a feminist and fantastic man by my side, who has taken care of our daughter as much as I have. He also runs several businesses and has always been very supportive. As well as work, children, friends and relations are a natural part of our life.

Iris van Herpen A/W 2010

Ramón Gurillo A/W 2010

Basso & Brooke A/W 2010

Justin Singh for Triumph International Award 2010

Basso & Brooke A/W 2010

ETHICAL FASHION DESIGNERS:
TARA & JOANNE SCOTT

Tara Starlet

You take pride in a retro feel; do you reuse old patterns?

We have a collection of original patterns, including some that have come from my grandma and some that have been accumulated over years of antique market trawling. We take inspiration from these patterns, as well as pin-up paintings and old Hollywood movies. But all of our designs are new and original.

Do you make any concessions to current fashion trends?

I wouldn't say we make concessions, but if for example there is a military trend (as there often is) we can take this and use it to help popularise our WWII suits and Land Army Dungarees. But the main drive is always our commitment to Vintage style.

Why did you decide to use only use recycled and end-of-roll fabric?

As a small business it is the easiest way to make sure that you are part of the cure rather than the cause when it comes to the negative environmental effects of the fashion industry. It is the perfect modern embodiment of the 1940's thrifty ethic of the Make Do and Mend era.

How do you set about reinventing the woolly jumper?

Every winter we do our upcycled cashmere cardigans, which we make using second hand cashmere jumpers. We chop off the neckline and make any necessary alterations to get a good fit, then put on a sweet faux-pony fur leopard print collar with a black satin bow. This allows us to give an old jumper that has been thrown away a very stylish new lease of life!

How many are you able to make of each design?

It depends, but we usually only get an average of about five garments in each size out of a particular fabric. This means that our designs are often just as exclusive as an original vintage piece.

What are the pros and cons of running the label as a mother-daughter team?

The dynamic can be difficult at times, but overall it works well because we both bring something different to the table. I have so much respect for my mother's knowledge of clothes making and fashion history, but she recognises that when it comes to running a modern business and connecting with a young fashion consumer I know what I'm talking about.

What are your plans for the future?

Our long-term dream is to evolve into a much more holistic ethical business. We would love to start using organic and fairtrade cotton, and have already made our first steps towards making that happen. I hope that one day we will be able to print our own textiles with eco dyes to recreate some of the amazing retro prints from our favourite decades. However this will obviously bump our prices up considerably and we do pride ourselves on providing affordable ethical fashion.

Tara Starlet S/S 2010

Andrea Peterson

self-portrait

Putting dreams in motion.

It's important - whether on a Brooklyn street corner or on top of a mountain at sunset - to collect beautiful moments of inspiration. I swim laps daily and find this is when I do my best thinking. I'll often work through an idea during my swims. This way, once I sit down to my painting, illustration, or sketch pad, I have had time to process - you could even say meditate - on all the inspirations I've encountered.

An idiosyncratic surrealist.

My paintings and drawings cover a wide range of styles so if I put two paintings of mine side by side you might not know they were by the same artist. But if you put ten pieces together in a room you would recognise the underlying style. It's a natural inclination to continue experimenting.

The nostalgia of Anja Hynynen.

I am currently following a nostalgic theme in my paintings, inspired by nostalgic World War-era grainy sepia photos, busty pin-up girls, and a past that no society has been able to escape: the toils and struggle of war, and the quest for peace, beauty and power. Anja Hynynen's flowing ethereal designs caught my eye because they have a similar old-world style, a Victorian flair in the detail, and I love her romantic use of white. They are feminine without being overtly so, which is how I like to draw my characters.

Fine art and illustration compliment each other.

I usually create sketches for my paintings, and these tend to have an illustrative, narrative quality to them. Sometimes I do an illustration, then create a larger and more elaborate painting from it. For me, fine art and illustration go hand in hand, and I constantly learn and develop my style from the differences in each process.

Learning it all.

Art was not a choice for me, but a path that felt natural. In any school, you absorb information congruently to how passionate you are in your field of study and East Carolina University prepared me very well for the world of commercial art. Not to say that school was easy! It was very challenging for me, especially because I wanted to learn and experiment with everything: graphic design, printmaking, illustration, and oil painting. I chose to major in Commercial Illustration but I also took as many painting classes as I could, sometimes completing my illustrations as oil paintings (who says the two worlds don't blend?) I had wonderful,

Inspired by her romantic and dreamy style I asked Arizona-based artist Andrea Peterson to create the wonderful image for the cover of this book. She looks very like one of her paintings, willowy, with a heart shaped face and long hair, a fact which she puts down to ease of reference and her sister, who looks similar, having modelled for her at times. Currently working part time in a gallery, she shares her studio with Frida the adopted chihuahua, chosen from the rescue centre in part because she bears the name of Frida Kahlo, her favourite artist. "She's my little buddy, she sits on my lap when I'm painting." Andrea often cycles to work with Frida strapped into a harness in her bike basket.

Missoni A/W 2010

Missoni S/S 2010

Cecilia Mary Robson S/S 2011

Charlie Le Mindu S/S 2011

talented teachers - all of whom were amazing and driven artists themselves, which was also inspiring. I was taught the significance of copyright, contracts, and keeping an updated website, which are definitely important in this field. I was lucky to have learned these aspects early on.

From New York to Arizona.
I lived in New York City for several years so I could be amidst the art scene after university. It was a whirlwind time when I made some amazing connections and I still have a gallery there, but after several years I felt cramped with my lack of studio space so I followed a friend to Arizona. I quickly found a job at a gallery and had much more space to paint and enjoy the sunny western landscape of mountains and cactus. Of course I miss New York at times, so working closely with writers in London over London Fashion Week is great because I feel part of what's happening and what's fresh in a huge metropolitan city. It's an exciting process to receive emailed photos straight from the runway and then immediately create illustrations from them.

Creating a fashion illustration.
First, I begin by splattering watercolour paper with watercolours or inks. I usually do this to several pieces of paper at a time and then study them as they dry, turning them different ways to see how the illustration I have in mind would fit. Starting with abstract splatters or a toned background is the most exciting way to begin an illustration. Once I decide on a position, I sketch directly on the paper in pencil, working lightly, so I can erase here and there; once I like the drawing, I darken and define my pencil lines. Then I go in with watercolour touches and the black ink comes last, to define the figure and clothing. Once it is dry I apply touches of white gouache to accent the figure and clothing if necessary; or I may do this digitally. The end! Obviously, the process varies here and there, but these are my typical steps.

Facebook clicks.
Discovering Amelia's Magazine was one of those serendipitous things. I found it through Facebook and was immediately intrigued. One click led to another, I read a couple of articles and thought it would be a great idea to get involved. I'd been thinking of expanding my fashion illustration portfolio, so it got me on the right track. When I decide to do something I tend to go full force.

Faster, chihuahua.
The quick turn-around time for the magazine has helped me develop a fast watercolour style and my composition decision-making skills have sharpened. As for working from Arizona, U.S. I might not get as much sleep as I would like but I do now keep London time on my computer. In some way it's a perk to be able to work overnight. Deadlines are deadlines; freelance work in New York prepared me well for keen communication skills in a virtual environment. Creating the cover for Amelia's Compendium of Fashion Illustration really pushed me to balance my creativity with specific art direction and it was wonderful to work so closely with Amelia in this process.

Next for Artist Andrea.
I'm wrapping up my Nostalgia series of paintings and submitting new works to galleries. I hope to participate in more group shows, gain gallery representation in Los Angeles and possibly in London too. I would love any excuse to visit... and perhaps linger for several months since I have relatives there! I'm also working on a children's book in my spare time, and keeping an eye on community-based art projects in other countries, such as Wide Open Walls, where a group of artists have painted murals across an entire village in Gambia, Africa. I am excited by any opportunity that blends travel, art, and working closely with a community.

David Koma
S/S 2011

Spijkers en Spijkers S/S 2011

Ute Decker

Ethical jeweller Ute Decker makes "wearable sculptures" that can be inhabited and interacted with – actively influencing an evolving aesthetic and sensuous experience. She is one of the first jewellers to receive a licence to work with certified fairtrade gold.

Your first degree was in political economics and you led an extremely interesting life before becoming a jeweller. What prompted the move into jewellery?

Making jewellery started out as a hobby with evening classes nearly ten years ago. A combination of upheaval in my private life, a period of being unwell and the enthusiastic response to my work encouraged me to indulge my creative passion and take on a new challenge. I decided to change career and become a full-time jeweller in 2009. The time since then has been hard work but thoroughly rewarding.

How has being a journalist given you a more enquiring mind and what worries you most?

Journalists must be able to research, ask questions, challenge views, separate facts from spin and analyse information within an historical, social, political as well as environmental context. These same skills helped me immensely when facing the very steep learning curve of a new jeweller striving to work ethically. What worries me is that jewellers are taught technical and conceptual skills without knowledge of the wider social and environmental context of their craft. Fortunately ethical jewellery makers are raising awareness of these issues and this is slowly changing. I believe the jewellery industry will look rather different in a very short space of time. The high profile launch of certified fairtrade gold - with a completely transparent supply chain from mine to jewellery box - will increase the already growing awareness and help jewellers as well as consumers to make more informed choices.

How does your collaboration with CRED work?

Cred is a pioneering ethical jeweller and fairtrade precious metal supplier. We are both engaged in raising awareness, creating and promoting ethical jewellery. Cred supplies my recycled silver as well as stocking my work in their Chichester boutique.

You have also worked in sculpture, textiles, paper and ceramics. How on earth have you managed to do all of this?

These are all related, all equally enjoyable creative outlets for me. Each discipline informs and enriches the others. I am enthusiastic about so-called livelong learning; each year from the age of about twelve I have taken one or several courses – from art history to Zen buddhism, from basketry via philosophy to textiles. It is amazing what you can learn and where such learning may lead you.

What do you do to relax?

Relax?! For the last eighteen months my life has centred around crafting and promoting ethical jewellery. Workaholic tendencies are certainly most useful when starting a new career... I find a good game of squash or badminton invigorating as well as relaxing and the occasional long country walks help to recharge my batteries and put the challenges and petty nuisances of a hectic London city life back into perspective. Hopefully soon I will have time again to enjoy music, contemporary dance, theatre, reading, lectures and evening classes more often. After all, many of these pleasures are the reason I live in London.

How has the Japanese practice of Wabi Sabi influenced your work practice?

Years ago a friend gave me a book on Wabi Sabi and I was amazed by how close the ethos of this ancient Japanese philosophy was to my own conscious and intuitive values and aesthetic. The concept was first coined by Sen Rikyu, the founder of the Japanese tea ceremony. At the time the sheer lavishness of the tea ceremony was designed to impress and in contrast Sen Rikyu suggested a style centred on beautiful minimalism. He proposed the elimination of all extraneous clutter in order to appreciate beauty in its simplest most essential form. Wabi Sabi is as much a philosophy or world view as a design aesthetic, and respect is an important part of the concept. Wabi Sabi promotes an intuitive feel for life, where relationships between people and their environments should be harmonious. It values a mindful presence in this world based on a sense of stewardship rather than ownership of nature.

Why are ethics and beauty so intertwined?

It may be an expression of love but a typical gold wedding band leaves in its wake on average twenty tons of waste laced with toxic chemicals. Many of the primary jewellery materials involve huge amounts of suffering and cruelty. Gold and gemstones have funded war lords in west Africa and propped up corrupt regimes in Zimbabwe and Burma. Jewellery manufacturing itself may involve further toxic chemicals and exploitative working conditions. I aim to make the beauty of my pieces integral; from the mindful choice of the materials' provenance through to the careful hand-crafting of each individual piece in my studio. Working ethically underpins the entire ethos and concept

Ute Decker

of my jewellery, so I exclusively work in 100% recycled silver, non-toxic bio-resin and soon in fairtrade gold. I believe we are as much sensory as cognitive creatures so I have long been interested in the relation between ethics and aesthetics in artefacts - you might call it the question of social beauty. Divorcing aesthetics from its moral dimension, the cult of beauty for beauty's sake is lacking an important, deeper dimension. Beauty as a material version of 'goodness' can teach and remind us about the qualities to which it alludes, such as love, trust, intelligence, kindness and justice. By having such works around us, we can be subtly reminded of the constituents of virtue. This is particularly true for jewellery, which we wear directly on our body as symbols of love or to express our individuality, and in the broadest sense to promote our sense of well-being. By working ethically as a jeweller I strive to acknowledge this complex relationship between beauty and ethics, between outer beauty and inner beauty. With growing awareness of the ethical issues associated with jewellery, this moral interconnectedness is an increasingly urgent question for anyone making jewellery today.

Why do you think it's important to share your resources with others?

It was initially extremely difficult and time consuming to find out about less socially and environmentally damaging alternatives to standard jewellery practice, so now I am happy to share this information in articles, seminars and on my website, where I include background articles, fact sheets and a list of suppliers. For me striving to work ethically as a jeweller is not about being holier than thou or asserting a business advantage, it is about genuinely wanting to improve the social and environmental impact of my own work and that of the jewellery industry as a whole. This can best be achieved by sharing information, working together and supporting each other's efforts.

Charlotte Eskildsen S/S 2011

Chanel Cruise Line 2010

Jena Theo S/S 2011

Imogen Belfield A/W 2010

Coco de Mer

Lako Bukia S/S 2011

Anja Hynynen

Gabby Young tour poster ›

Cecilia Mary Robson S/S 2011

Anja Hynynen

ETHICAL FASHION DESIGNER

Anja Hynynen

How has a love of arts and handicrafts been passed down to you?

Amongst my ancestors there is a menswear tailor, a well-known Swedish painter, and my three aunts who worked with textiles. My father keeps a family tradition alive as a blacksmith and my mother is an artisan working with leather and photography. Since finding my passion within drawing, textile and environment it feels natural to follow my heart. I wish more people were able to work with what they feel is important.

What prompted you to start working with organic fabrics?

I became allergic to some fabrics when I begun to sew full-time, and getting sick made me wonder about the health of the people and the soil in the places where those fabrics were being grown, woven and dyed, as well as what happens to the water in which we wash these toxic clothes at home. I grew up close to nature, and experiencing first hand the fallout from poisonous chemicals made me want to search for pure materials to create ethical clothing.

Where do you source your organic materials from?

I find the background of materials fascinating. It's so important to understand where fabrics come from; to be able to tell a customer the story, from seed to finished garment. I work with organic wool, linen, cotton, hemp and peace silk. The linen is grown and woven in Germany and Austria, where it is certified the whole way through production. For detailed artistic work such as felting I like to work with local materials such as handspun angora rabbit yarn and native sheep wool; materials where I have the opportunity to know the source personally. One of my dreams would be to ensure the local production of materials that we can produce in this part of the world, such as wool, hemp and linen fabrics.

How is finding a new organic textile producer a bit like detective work?

I do a lot of research, which leads me to people who are doing wonderful work with animals, land and fabric, both near and far. This means that I have beautiful material with which to make my collections. It used to be very hard to find organic textiles so it is a joy to see the market growing: each time someone asks for ethical fabrics the more there will be to choose from. I always keep my eyes open.

How will you transfer what you have learnt to local producers and artisans in Sweden?

I hope my fashion designs show the possibility of combining beauty and arts with respect for nature - inspiring sustainable thinking in any kind of field. Everything we do makes rings on the water so I am happy to talk about my work and exchange my knowledge with others. I am currently arranging an organic textiles art project; the purpose being to bring people together to create something beautiful, offer advice on where to find materials and spread the word for a more environmentally friendly future.

What inspires the way you design?

Although there are some signature details and cuts which appear in all my garments I don't work with seasonal trends, instead producing timeless designs in one constantly evolving collection. I recently did a show that featured organic evening and bridal wear and it included tailored corsets, draped and flexible dresses which can be changed from full length into shorter cocktail dresses to increase the wearability. Many of my clothes are made to measure specifically for the customer, and a selection is available through my website.

What kind of natural dyes do you use?

I am fascinated by natural dyes and the special qualities of their colours. I work with a lot of local leaves and flowers, some of which are wild and some that are grown in the garden. I derive the colours by boiling the plants in a wood-fired barrel or by letting them soak in cold water for slower processes. The quality of the water, material of the boiling pot or the soil where the plants grew can all play a part in the final colour. We have a lot of birch trees, which give yellow shades and a recent experiment produced a gorgeous dark purple from St. John's Wort that I hope to use for an evening dress.

How does being Swedish affect your attitude to clothing and design?

I don't necessarily feel Swedish because I don't see borders: most of all I feel like a member of the world. But I love the surroundings where I live; they give constant inspiration and materials to work with, and I think this enables me to make clothes that are personal, unique, beautiful and that people feel good wearing. Where possible, production of clothes should be local to the people who wear the clothes, but organic clothing should be for everyone, no matter what part of the world they live in.

Aniela Murphy

FASHION ILLUSTRATOR

Your degree was in fine art; why have you pursued a career in graphic design and illustration?

Fine Art seemed the obvious choice to me when I was eighteen and all I wanted to do was paint and draw, but then I wasn't really aware of the other course options that were available... at that point, as with many school leavers, the next three years WAS the rest of my life as far as I was concerned; anything beyond that seemed irrelevant and too far in front to give a second thought. I regret not going on an Art Foundation course because it set me behind in terms of specialising and knowing myself as an artist, which stunted my confidence and ability to develop creatively and bridge that infamous gap between A Level and degree level. Only when I did a collaborative project with a friend that included some illustration, did I realise that I prefer to problem solve a brief rather than set it. This set the ball in motion and it hasn't stopped since.

What has your fine art background brought to the subject?

At university I learned more about what doesn't work for me rather than what does, so more than anything I've learned from my mistakes. For example, when I'm in a creative rut I just carry on producing work until something clicks - if I sit back it becomes dead time. The majority of my first year was spent researching theories of aesthetics rather than actually producing anything of value and I didn't feel comfortable with the work I was making - I was trying to make a bold statement rather than focus on quality. If I'm blunt and incredibly honest, I don't think I grew at university as an artist, but I did learn more about myself.

How have you learnt what is required of an illustrator?

Just under a year ago I had very little knowledge of the illustration world but I became pretty determined to find out more so I have been reading and researching ever since. There have been disadvantages, but finding out about things myself has made me more of a go-getter than I ever thought possible. I sometimes struggle with pricing because I don't negotiate as hard as I could, but these things come with experience as your confidence grows. The business side of things is totally new to me so I went on a few courses, but have had to apply what I learned to my own situation without any illustration-specific guidance. Even without a tutor as a mentor I know I've come so far already and I can't wait to see what is to come.

What is it that attracts you to fashion illustrations and how have you developed?

I taught myself to draw people using fashion magazines when I was young and I remember the moment that I cracked it at about twelve years old. I still examine the poses in magazines for inspiration and I guess it just feels very appealing: familiar and comfortable. I always start at the drawing board because my love of drawing made me want to be a visual artist in the first place, plus I don't want to be sucked into the digital age too fast - there's often no way back. With fashion photography as a reference point I digitally draw and paint over my original artwork to bring separate elements together, sometimes creating hand

self-portrait

drawn borders to tessellate around the edges. Because illustration is a relatively new world to me my method is still evolving, and contributing to Amelia's Magazine has given me an incredible opportunity to develop creatively.

What are the staples of your studio set up?

My computer is pretty key, since most things tend to stem from it. I work alone at the moment, so it's like a portal to the outside world. I have my camera and my scanner close by, and a large table covered with various sized sketchbooks, a pile of fashion, illustration and digital art magazines that I can flick through when I need an inspiration lift, and my stationary box filled with pens, pencils and Poscas. My kettle is pretty important, and I always have milk and a loaf of bread nearby in case I get really into a piece of work and forget to eat properly. It's rare but it does happen.

Why does imaginative typography inspire you?

One of my favourite books is Handwritten: Expressive Lettering in the Digital Age by Steven Heller. I love it so much because it reminds you to start at the drawing board, never to lose sight of manual drawing in this digital age. Visually it is absolutely wonderful, full of raw yet fluid hand rendered lettering examples.

As an enthusiastic social networker, which platforms do you enjoy using for what things?

Twitter has been an incredible resource over the past year and I think of it as the professional social network. I love the illustration community on there and I have become acquainted with some fantastic creative individuals; illustrators, designers and art directors, who offer me advice and feedback when needed. It's a great way of finding out about creative opportunities, and so easy to link up to other great sites like Flickr and Society6. For me Facebook is more of a way of keeping touch with old friends but I do have an artist fan page because you never know when the next door is going to open!

What inspired you to draw ethical designers?

I think ethical fashion is something that everyone needs to think about since we all wear clothes. I admire the work of designers who strive to make something beautiful and ethically sound in an industry that has been notoriously cruel in the past. What's the point in clothes that make you look and feel good if you have endorsed the poor treatment of factory workers or harmed the environment during production? So it is brilliant to be able to highlight how and where clothes are made through my illustration.

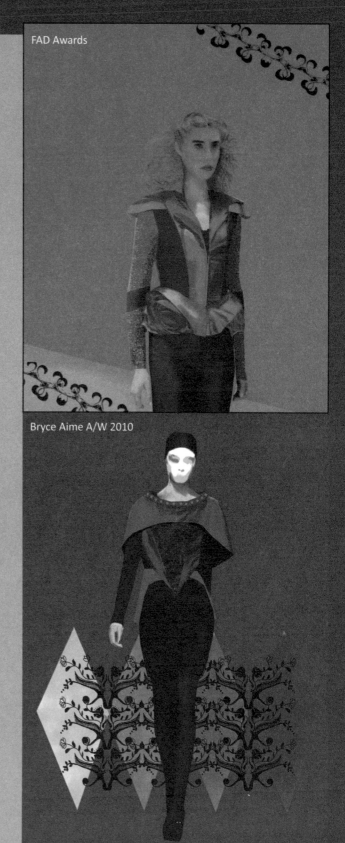

FAD Awards

Bryce Aime A/W 2010

Bunmi Koko S/S 2011

KTZ S/S 2011

Junky Styling

ETHICAL FASHION DESIGNERS:
ANNIKA SANDERS & KERRY SEAGER

Annika Sanders and Kerry Seager are self-taught fashion designers. They started up Junky Styling after they received lots of compliments for their deconstructed and restyled secondhand suits made to go out clubbing in during the 1990's.

What prompted your approach to dressmaking?

Our approach was initially borne out of a lack of money but it soon became a necessity for individuality and quality. At first Annika's mother did most of the sewing so our designs were heavily directed by her.

Have you seen many changes over the years?

Aside from all the wrinkles on our faces? We have seen the tangible development of a marketplace that never existed before. Education has enabled the sustainable movement to become more widely accepted and understood, and now many new brands think about sustainability before they even start designing.

Where did you go out in the past and do you still go clubbing?

We went to a wide mixture of venues that hosted a similar dressy scene. It was such a brilliant time, and we still enjoy socialising and a bit of a shuffle. But we always try to ensure that we are not the oldest at the bar.

Why did you set up business in Brick Lane?

We traded from a space in Kensington Market for several months prior to the opening of our shop here, which was nearly fifteen years ago. We were lucky enough to know one of the guys behind the redevelopment of the Old Truman Brewery.

Can you explain the process behind the Wardrobe Surgery?

Wardrobe Surgery was organically born whilst we were still trading at Kensington Market. We encourage people to bring us their most treasured items from the back of their wardrobes - pieces that they are no longer wearing but can't bear to part with for whatever reason - and we refashion them according to the customer's desires. We specialise in prolonging the life of clothes, allowing details and memories of a much-loved outfit to continue as an active part of a customer's life.

How do you ensure continuity of design within orders when you are recycling different clothing all the time?

The Estethica exhibition at London Fashion week is a perfect platform to facilitate sales to small boutiques. Trust plays a large part in our working relationships because buyers are often buying blind, but our steady clients know that we always use the highest quality fabrics. Our wholesale range is available in a range of sizes and colour options that are decided when an order is placed, but clients are tolerant of a bit of diversity. For example, if an order is placed for dark striped dresses they will tend to arrive in many different versions of chalk-stripe and pinstripe. Individuality, but still off-the-peg, has become a great selling point.

How can we persuade mainstream fashion to be less trend dependent?

The fashion industry is so massive that changes need to start at the very top, where trends are decided months if not years in advance. But do we really need to stop trends? I think it is more important to consider the way that garments are produced. My biggest wish for change within mainstream fashion is that transparency should become the norm.

Junky Styling S/S 2010

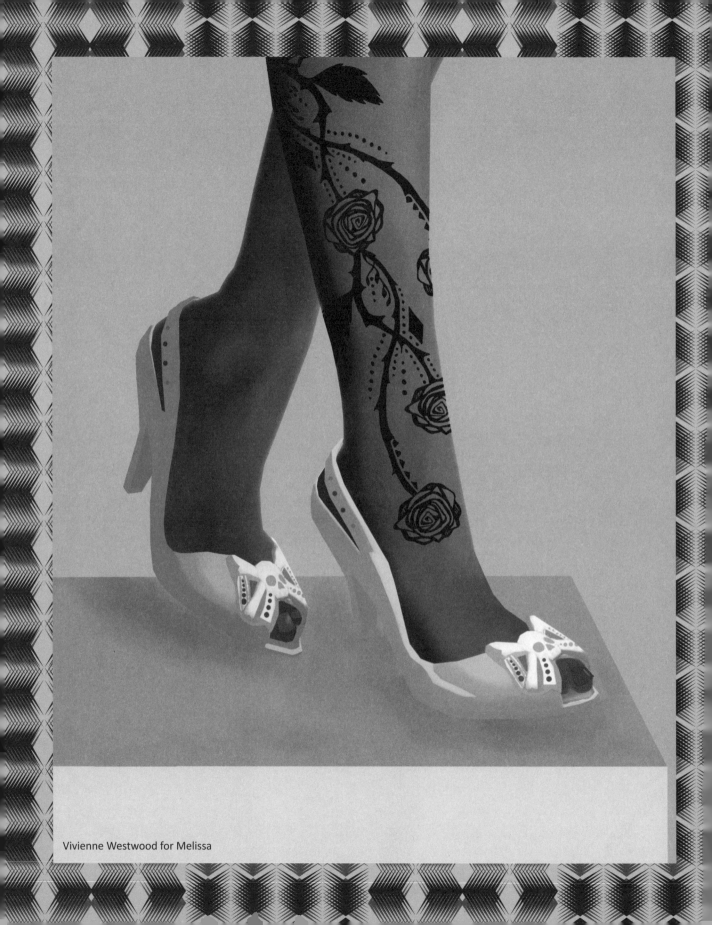

Vivienne Westwood for Melissa

Morgan Allen Oliver S/S 2011

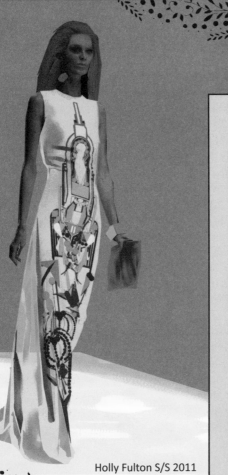

Holly Fulton S/S 2011

Holly Fulton S/S 2011

Morgan Allen Oliver S/S 2011

061

Jenny Robins

Your illustrations have the most amazing energy - how do you produce them?

Where possible, I like to work from a lot of different sources – so I'll have lots of photos open on my computer at once or I will pause video to capture movement. Even if I'm working from a single image I still try to maintain the feel of live drawing by looking at individual elements within the whole, and drawing really quickly with ink or paint. I've done a lot of live drawings of musicians and catwalk shows where there is only a few moments to capture a pose or an outfit, and this feeds back into my illustration work with an attitude of less is more. I always do the face and figure quickly and I think the energy comes from combining rapid gestural drawing with more considered details.

self-portrait

What attracts you to fashion illustration?

When I was younger I had a very experimental dress sense: I wore lots of tutus and novelty hats. Nowadays I suffer from serious shoe envy. I am really fascinated by how catwalk fashion trickles down to the high street - they are weirdly separate and yet interrelated. Fashion with a big F is about creating fantasy and spectacle, and illustration can run with that idea and show designs in a more imaginative way than photography can. And I get to draw things that are both dynamic and pretty. Which is nice.

Why is it important to promote ethical fashion as an attractive proposition?

Our perception of fashion as a right not a privilege has become a little warped; it's easy to see cheap sweat shop fashion as a win-win situation: starving kids get a few pence towards not starving and over-worked (relatively) under-paid western women gain a few hours of feeling less depressed thanks to a new pair of shoes. But no-one really wins. The shoes will most likely fall apart. There are a lot of middle market clothing chains that aren't much better quality than the lower end of the market, nor do they have a better ethical stamp on them - so if we're not paying for better quality or ethics then what are we paying for? Many people have an outdated idea of ethical fashion as hippyish or expensive but that's not necessarily true, and knowing you've done the right thing is way more fulfilling than just having new shoes. The main problem is lack of exposure about the issues; the more that people know, the more they will demand ethical behaviour as the norm from high street retailers... much like free range eggs.

You also write - how do you think words and pictures complement each other?

Words and pictures can enhance each other's meaning when put together. I think fashion illustrations are even better than photographs in this context as there is more communicative potential. Likewise when communicating an issue or idea the right words are very important to anchor an image's meaning.

What inspired you to start your Facebook project, drawing all your friends in alphabetical order?

I love having a long term project to keep me grounded, and the Facebook project relates to a lot of areas I find interesting: cultural studies, personal image, social dynamics, social networking, you know, post modern life and stuff. It's a very social project that allows me to connect with friends old and new and remember how much I love people. It keeps me challenged because I try to use lots of different styles, and some people have actively participated to request a certain style. Of course some friends are not on Facebook which boggles my mind - it's as if they don't exist but of course they do! The project has been going in fits and starts as I'm so busy in the manner of a bee, but when I don't have other illustration work to do it's great to have some drawing to get on with.

Why have you decided to pursue a career in art and design teaching and how is this affecting the way you produce illustrations?

Well, obviously when I was applying for the course I didn't say I was attempting to secure a steady income... but seriously, teaching is a properly fulfilling and challenging adventure that I'm really enjoying. The idea is to become financially stable but I'm also a very social butterfly, I mean person, and I would go a bit mad if I just sat alone in my room freelancing, so the aim is to balance the two. I also want to indoctrinate the next generation.

What kind of stuff do you sell on Etsy?

I mostly sell cards, prints and zines, like my zine What Birds are Really Thinking - which is a really hot topic and everyone should know about it. I have a semi-separate 'fine art' practice where I just paint birds a lot. It's fine art because the images aren't done to a brief, and sometimes the birds get exhibited in galleries. I also sell stuff that I made just because I had an idea, and left over items from when I had a market stall - which was very time intensive but very fun: I recommend it.

Why are politics important to you and why do you think that illustration is important in transmitting ideas?

I started illustrating political ideas for Amelia's Magazine in response to the information that was flooding in on Twitter. I guess politics are important to me because politics are important, if you get me. And illustration can be used to get key issues and viewpoints across easily; I often read the cartoons in the paper rather than the words because I don't have time. Good political illustrators can

turn around a concept in a short time frame, where the equivalent in photography form might be unreliable or uncommunicative. A good political illustrator can also make people question their assumptions.

What do you hope for in the future?

I have all the lottery dreams of self-publishing, running a gallery/studio/cafe/bar/shop/venue where I get all the coolest undiscovered talent and sell affordable tea and yummy cake and ethical fashions. Maybe I'll get there, but I'll be happy just to keep drawing and teaching and making friends. For the world, I just hope that the people who make the big decisions somehow miraculously have the capacity to see the big picture. Or maybe they need to paint a smaller picture. How's that for an obtuse political metaphor?

You're very prolific - how do you manage to find time to work on illustrations?

I cut back on non essential activities. Like washing. Not really. People have always told me I am prolific but I don't really see it. Part of being a creative person in today's hectic job scene means that you have to grab everything that comes your way, and I am interested in most things... apart from Formula One Racing. If I wasn't illustrating or painting for part of the week, I would be really grumpy. It's more of an effort to not draw. I see things I want to draw everywhere when I don't have time to stop and draw them, and have ideas for projects and pictures I don't have time to do. So for myself, I do not feel prolific.

Doii A/W 2010

Paul Costelloe A/W 2010

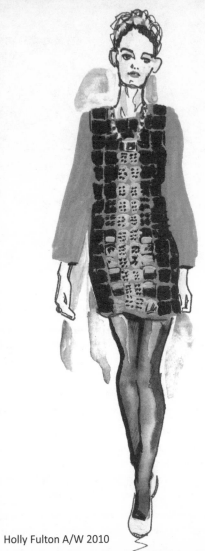

Holly Fulton A/W 2010

Frances Conteh S/S 2011

You've been going for a very long time. Have attitudes to ethical fashion started to change yet?

Consumers are starting to question the huge exploitation of people and the environment that permits their clothing to be so cheap, because it doesn't add up. There is still a long way to go but the fashion industry is slowly changing the way it does business.

What has the People Tree brand achieved?

We support 5,000 farmers, artisans and their families in developing countries by producing well designed fairtrade and sustainable products. For us it's about creating sustainable livelihoods that put food on the table at the end of the day.

You've collaborated with both Bora Aksu and Karen Nichol. What have they brought to People Tree?

We've worked with Bora for four years because we share the view that good fashion design should last for years. He is a master of beautiful, feminine draped designs that we produce in organic and fairtrade cotton, and we've already started designing an exciting new collection for S/S 2012. Like me Karen is passionate about handicrafts and she loves traditional Japanese textiles and designs. She works with our hand knitters in Nepal to create beautiful appliquéd and hand embroidered embellishments.

Why did you choose to work with actress Emma Watson?

We were introduced by a friend and clicked instantly because Emma is intelligent and passionate about promoting fairtrade amongst her own age group. She is totally committed to her collection: to fit design meetings around her busy filming schedule we work late into the night. And we have a similar design aesthetic, so working together is fun.

Why are designer collaborations and celebrity endorsement so important?

We like to work with people who are passionate about skills and really understand what fairtrade is all about. We also have a team of People Tree ambassadors – key fashion opinion leaders such as Laura Bailey and Livia Firth. Henry Holland would be fun to collaborate with. We could create some amazing message tees to celebrate People Tree's 20th anniversary in Japan and our 10th in the UK.

How do you intend to celebrate twenty years in the business?

We will have lots of fairtrade organic chocolate fountain parties in both Japan and the UK. We're also working together with our fairtrade groups to create some wonderful new products to showcase and celebrate their skills. It will be a busy year. I hope that in the next twenty years values of sustainability and social justice become the norm. This economic system is in need of a huge shake up – roll on Mayan change of 2012.

People Tree S/S 2011

People Tree S/S 2011

Pam Hogg A/W 2010

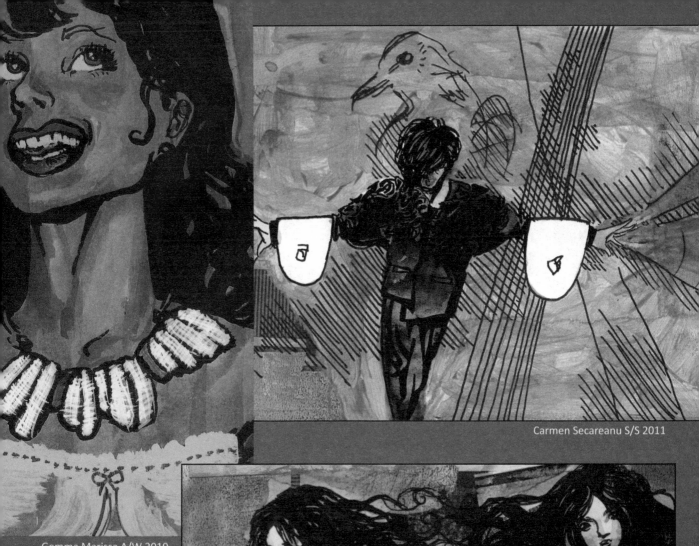

Carmen Secareanu S/S 2011

Gemma Marissa A/W 2010

Biba S/S 2011

Alexxsia Elizabeth Graduate Collection 20

Paul Costelloe A/W 2010

Sabrina Miller Graduate Collection 2010

Nicola Roberts

Emma Block

FASHION ILLUSTRATOR

self-portrait

Emma Block has only been creating fashion illustrations since she got involved with Amelia's Magazine, the open briefs enabling her to find her feet and develop her style, which encompasses collaging, painting, etching and screen printing. She assembles the component parts of cut paper and then paints highlights on the skin and other areas before scanning the artwork into her computer. Putting pen or paint brush to paper feels too definite, but with cut paper Emma can endlessly rearrange, trying new colourways, backgrounds and compositions, avoiding the need for black lines. It's a style that suits her love of pattern and attention to detail. She uses paper that has already had a previous life such as paper bags, envelopes, flyers or wrapping paper. Pages from old books have the perfect weight, texture and absorbency as well as a beautiful patina. Not only does Emma use lots of recycled materials, but she also wears lots of second hand clothes; being sustainable is hugely important to her.

Emma has kept a blog since the tender age of sixteen, at first to write down her thoughts - mainly about her dog - but she soon realised that she got the most feedback when she also posted drawings. The encouragement she gets from the online community, for instance when contributing to websites such as Illustration Friday, is hugely inspirational. Since an early age she has sold prints and other original work on Etsy and nowadays presents herself online in a very professional manner, so much so that she has been commissioned by several high-profile companies, including Woodmansterne, Time Out and Chronicle Books, all while still at college. All of these offers have been as a result of her internet presence, so she is constantly surprised to discover other students who have not yet engaged with the online world. She believes that leaving university is scary enough as it is, so the more you prepare yourself the better, especially when it comes to dealing with paying clients. Since it takes a while to build up an internet presence it's best to start while you still have the luxury of time on your side. She's already well aware that to be a successful illustrator she needs not only to be hugely creative but also to be very organised and business-like, which the experience of working on a university zine has taught her.

As a university student living in London she finds inspiration from visiting museums, art galleries and people-watching. She fills her room with inspiration: a huge collection of beautiful old illustrated books and postcards, all sorts of vintage ephemera. And a nice slice of cake can also help.

Catherine Feeny

Prada S/S 2010

YSL

DECORATIVE GRASSES 109

Vintage Patisserie

Marina and the Diamonds

Benefit makeover

Oria

ETHICAL JEWELLERY DESIGNERS:
TANIA KOWALSKI & SYNNOVE SAELTHUN

Tania Kowalski was a workshop manager at a well-known contemporary jewellery gallery in London when Synnove Saelthun arrived from New York to join the design team. They soon discovered that they had similar views on design and business ethics, and became good friends. Several years later they started the Oria brand, using Synnove's design skills and Tania's production expertise. Synnove is a technically brilliant goldsmith with a passion for design and an eye for detail. Tania is a trained jeweller, with a wide range of experience in the jewellery industry, from design creation through to production. Her expertise includes sourcing ethical materials and ensuring fair business practice.

Tania's passion for other cultures has led her to visit remote tribes in the Amazon of Brazil, hill tribes in Nepal and the Dogon people of Mali. It was during these travels that she became fascinated with the cultural importance and symbolic meaning of tribal adornment. When designing a new collection, the couple sit down together to discuss what the new collection will symbolise. They research and refine story boards, and after ensuring that the designs are technically feasible Synnove makes an initial prototype, the best of which will go into production.

The use of the phoenix is a symbol of honesty and justice in Chinese mythology, and is one of the inspirations for the Nina collection. The lotus symbolises purity and beauty in many different cultures, and it inspired their silver lotus collection.

Working in Nepal Tania discovered that the safe working conditions and fair living wages which we take for granted in the West are not necessarily the norm in other parts of the world. This early experience was important in persuading Tania to commit to fairtrade sourcing as a founding principle of Oria.

Doing this is one of the most challenging aspects of running the business. Standard large-scale mining typically uses toxic substances such as cyanide and mercury for extracting metal from rock ore. If these substances are not responsibly disposed of they can leak into the surrounding environment and the resulting pollution can destroy the land, harming plants, animals and people.

It took Oria over a year to source and ensure that all their metal and gems come from fairtrade sources, and they are continually looking for new sources of gemstones. They support the Kimberley Process, an initiative designed to stem the flow of rough 'blood diamonds' typically used by rebel movements to finance devastating conflicts in countries such as Angola and Sierra Leone.

They try to source diamonds from Canada and Australia because these countries are comparatively wealthy and are able to implement strict environmental and employment laws. Many of their suppliers work closely with mining communities to ensure that land rehabilitation, water filtration systems and solar energy projects are funded by ethical mining.

Synnove loved working in New York because New Yorkers are willing to spend whatever it takes to get what they want: as a result she worked with amazing gemstones, beads and rare pearls. America is ahead when it comes to the ethical market, but when it comes to design nothing beats London for excitement. Oria has private customers from the USA who love the 'London feel' of their designs.

Almost all their jewellery is made in Oria's London workshop, but they also use local specialists such as casters, laser cutters and stone setters when necessary. The finished pieces are stocked in a wide range of boutiques and jewellery galleries throughout the UK and online. They also make bespoke one-off pieces for private clients. Oria's hope is that, as more people become concerned with ethical business practices, existing suppliers will be motivated to work towards better ethical standards in their mines.

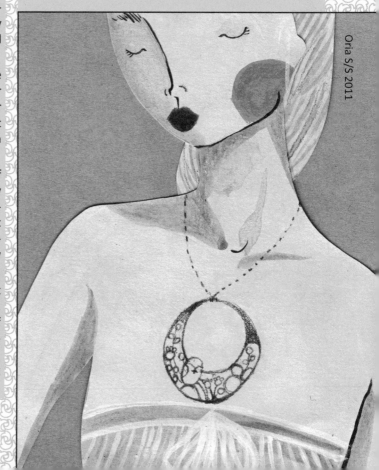

Oria S/S 2011

Lu Flux A/W 2010
Dame & Knight

PARTIMI S/S 2011
Dieu Bleu

Antonia Parker

Why do you describe yourself as a handmade illustrator and maker?

I've never been interested in making art on computers. I studied on a graphic design course that specialised in illustration, which meant that I soaked up the rules of graphic design, but the idea of spending hours on InDesign never seduced me. The balance between graphic and more illustrative styles in my class was quite evenly balanced, so whilst I was pushed forward in my development, my tutors and fellow students always supported the handcrafted element of my work. I basically rely on technology mostly for the scanning of my work and promoting it on the internet. I can't connect with something behind a screen, I want to touch it and get involved and make it myself. Even my camera is manual; I have to faff around with the film to make sure it doesn't jam. Making things generally involves getting covered in paint, pen, and bits of thread.

How do you work?

I draw in pencil and then on acetate in permanent marker because I find it gives the work a nice shiny effect. I then fill in the image from the back with interesting patterns and colour with acrylic paint and collage. In terms of how long an illustration takes, my body works to the speed of the deadline! I will somehow find the time to finish even if I need to make three pictures in the evening after work. I very much want to be drawing.

What kind of techniques did you learn on your illustration degree at LCC?

Obviously at the former London College of Printing we had access to great printmaking facilities, so I was able to explore all kinds of screen and relief-printing methods and there was a whole workshop devoted to letterpress. Not only were the technicians fantastic in passing on their knowledge, but they were really encouraging of our experimentation once we'd learnt the proper processes. I really enjoyed making photograms, taking materials of varied opacities down to the darkroom to make interesting images I could use in later illustrations. It meant that we didn't just print out an image for every project, but actually thought through the relevancy of our final outcomes. I was

always very envious of the true print-makers though; I'm much too messy for the perfect print!

What other things do you enjoy making?

What originally attracted me to studying illustration was that it could be anything that is drawn, even a 3D sculpture. Illustration is all around us. But for the purposes of describing my work I am not a pure illustrator. For example, my final collection at LCC consisted of heavily embellished costumes decorated in hand-done illustrations and typography on acetate as well as collaged Polaroids. I like to produce work in a variety of media because experimenting and trying new techniques keeps my work fresh and helps me to develop as an artist. I'm a manual person, I'm a maker. Whilst it's great to refine a method of working, I don't want my style to become too stilted. I'm an illustrator and I make costumes and sometimes I'm a photographer or printmaker. I work best when I have lots of work going on, because I become determined not to repeat myself. Artists like to differentiate themselves and no matter what I'm making, what all my work has in common is my sense of fun.

Where do you live and why?

When I lived in London I had access to all the latest exhibitions, both those of big names and of my colleagues, as well as plenty of art house cinema. It also meant I was brilliantly placed for internships and art jobs. However, this has all changed for me quite recently because I got married and moved down to Tunbridge Wells with my husband. I love walking through the green spaces to work instead of squeezing onto the tube, but it's not the same as being an artist in London. Living there was part of my identity as an illustrator – no one here cares about what I get up to outside my paid work, they just want their sandwich made nicely. I do a good Soup-of-the-Day board though.

How does your location impact your illustration practice?

Although Tunbridge Wells doesn't have much of an art scene, I recently had a stall at the first local Zine Fair, organised by one of my friends who also studied at the University of the Arts London. I ran a handmade 'photo booth' made lovingly from reclaimed cardboard, where I sat inside and drew my customers when they put money in the tinfoil coin slot. Having drawn their picture, I pushed it out through a slot-hole in the side of the booth as though it had been 'developed'. It felt great to be part of a new community and it's always healthy to do a bit of live illustration; it keeps you on your toes because the audience is right there. Otherwise work is pretty much the same as it's always been - sending my pictures to clients via email. Because I share a very small space with my husband it means a bit of co-operation and understanding when one of us is busy during the other's downtime. However, I'm happy, I have enough time to draw outside work and am gradually working on the personal projects that will take my illustrative career to the next stage.

What does your collective do?

When I left college it seemed impossible to find any work and almost as hard to find an internship, so my fellow LCC graduate Alia K Ahmad suggested that we put a website together to promote our fashion illustration. So, together with Holly Dinsdale and Adriana Munoz, we decided we'd collect together as a foursome to support and promote

each other's work through what can be a demoralising time. Drawing pictures means spending a lot of time on your own at a desk, so it is a great way to support each other and we are also able to pass more appropriate briefs on to one another. We didn't realise we would all soon disperse when we launched the London Fashion Illustration Collective website but we still spend time together drawing and working together when possible.

How has your ecological awareness impacted the way that you make artwork?

I am quite the hoarder — anytime I find an excitingly patterned paper or envelope, it gets tucked away for future use. As a result I often can't let go of things because I MIGHT use it! Obviously all art departments have to survive on low running costs, so throughout my education I've grown up trying not to waste materials. I also try to be a bit more responsible about what I use when making artwork, having been influenced by the utter lack of waste and re-using of materials when I interned with the brilliant Melanie Wilson, who runs the ecologically aware Prangsta Costumiers label on a tight budget. For my fashion illustrations I mostly use water-based acrylics on acetate, so whilst the production of the acetate and permanent markers unfortunately isn't so healthy, at least my paints are non-toxic and made in England.

You also enjoy making political illustrations - have you always been politically engaged?

I grew up in a very Conservative family in an agricultural area, so I was always aware of things from that angle. However, I've been interested in the Green Party since I was a teenager — in fact the best thing about voting in London was actually having a Green candidate. I'm now a member, as they seem to be the only humanely rational party. I have made a lot of work about political issues in the past, including sexual equality and female genital mutilation. Nobody makes political artwork because they're happy with a situation, it's because they're angry and want to reach out and change things.

How have you found the process of collaborating with Amelia's Magazine?

It's been really useful because people in the creative world know the magazine and really respect it. It means I've had a regular way to build up a good body of work to show off professionally and it has been good practice to have work that I need to get on with. It has been much more exciting than waiting for clients to come to me or just working on my own stuff and not knowing where it's going.

self-portrait

Mint Designs

Katie Eary S/S 2011 >

Felder Felder S/S 2011

Omar Kashoura
S/S 2011

By Stamo

By Stamo S/S 2010

Zoe Davidson Graduate Collection 2010

Simon Ekrelius S/S 2011

Wilfried Pletzinger A/W 2010

Wilfried Pletzinger

For sports enthusiast Wilfried Pletzinger it felt right to upcycle his favourite vintage style, sportswear. He cycles daily and swims several times a week - in the lake outside his house in Sweden during summer - so it was easy to start off his first collection by clearing out his own wardrobe. He aims to make sportswear sexy and wearable for party and evening wear so the challenging part has been giving clothes a new life in a new context. He designs for both genders, turning menswear into womenswear and vice versa.

Wilfried has spent twenty years styling and designing fashion collections as well as stage costumes for bands and dancers. He moved from Berlin to Sweden in 2000 to design for H&M, and after that fell into teaching design and production. A few years ago he felt the urge to express himself creatively under his own name again and that led to the birth of his new label.

He thinks it is still difficult to work commercially with upcycling, but that attitudes are changing fast. Swedes

are great at picking up the newest trends but they are not very courageous in expressing their personal style beyond those trends, so showing at Alternative Fashion Week in London gave him a great deal of publicity through articles in magazines and a variety of fashion websites and blogs. He also got some helpful new contacts, including that of an ethical stylist. He finds it easier to show in London, and in Berlin, where he hopes to move soon.

At the moment he produces one-off exclusive items directly from his workshop, so they are not available to a wide market. In the future he hopes to buy up whole stocks of unsold collections to upcycle. He will always use elements of sportswear but would like to combine this with other materials. Until recently he bought most of his clothes from flea markets or secondhand shops but he is currently in dialogue with one of the bigger sports brands about a collaboration.

Bolshie A/W 2010

Zandra Rhodes at FAD Awards

Hilary Alexander at LFW

WHO'S "OM BARGAIN PAYING FOR YOUR CHEAP CLOTHES?

Bolshie S/S 2011

Rachel de Ste. Croix

self-portrait

Why the nickname Precious Little?

I chose Precious Little partly because my real name is hard for people to pronounce and also because I liked the implied meaning - something small but treasured; both valued and valueless. I feel as if this is reflected in my work, and perhaps all art, to some extent. I put a lot of time and effort into my illustrations, and I hope that people enjoy them and connect with them on some level, but that said, all they do is make the world a prettier place. And Precious Little also sounds good.

Can you describe the life of a freelance illustrator?

Varied! Particularly as I also do a lot of design work as well as illustration. One day I might be laying out a children's book cover, the next I am drawing scantily clad ladies, or working on a private commission. Some weeks I may be working fourteen hour days, and others will be quiet. I was lucky to find a couple of 'bread and butter' clients quite soon after graduating, so I stuck with them for awhile and let self-promotion take a back seat until quite recently. That's starting to play a bigger role now, and seems to be paying off. There's also the boring side - self-assessment tax forms are not my favourite thing about this job.

What is the relationship between children's book illustration and fashion illustration?

It may sound strange, but I feel there is a natural crossover between my children's book illustration and my fashion illustration. I feel that the best of both are inventive, whimsical and do not take themselves too seriously. I enjoy reflecting a sense of dream-like playfulness in all my work. I think that a fashion illustration is better when there is an implied narrative of story or character, and it is more than just a picture of a pretty outfit. For me on obvious link would be the drawings on the front of Butterick and McCall's dress patterns - their job is to inspire the person sewing the outfit, but there's always a half-story in those pictures. Another example of the two crossing over would be in girls' comics of the kind you don't really see any more — the Jackie heroine beautifully drawn dressed to the nines, involved in a chaste romance with the boy of her dreams.

How do you create your fashion illustrations?

I start off by making sketches based on photographs of the designs, lightbox the best one and go over it more accurately in pencil. Then I go over that again in black pen or ink in further detail, and scan in the finished line-art. I like to work quite big so sometimes I have to painstakingly stitch two sides of an image together in Photoshop. I usually colour them digitally. I use large textured brushes and samples of scanned fabrics to build up the image layer by layer. I also like to offset the outlines, which gives the finished image an additional screen-printed effect. Although my line-art tends to be tight and very intricate, I like to keep the colouring style bright, loose and experimental. My aim is usually to re-imagine the original design in a way that is eye-catching, inviting and unusual. I try to ensure that my work never has the cold, overly slick look that digital art can sometimes have. When I have the time, I also enjoy working traditionally, using acrylic ink, watercolour and coloured pencils.

What exhibitions have you been involved in?
I recently had an exhibition on London's Brick Lane with some of my fellow Westminster graduates, and I've also done some 'one night only' exhibitions, as well as some live illustration at Sketchbook Magazine's pop-up real-time magazine. I definitely think that getting your work out of the studio, making personal connections and showing off your artistic colours is worth the effort – even if you sell little or nothing on first, second or third time, it will come back around to you. People remember you, come back to you, and may be biding their time before contacting you months later to offer new opportunities - so I'd say keep business cards and small purchases available if you can. It's all a learning experience, you just have to be willing to work hard and reassess the situation now and then. Getting out of the studio can also be refreshing and helps clear the cobwebs out of your brain. I definitely intend to keep doing exhibitions, and would also love to get involved in craft markets and selling directly to the public.

Do you have any other jobs?
I currently have a part-time job in a pharmacy, mostly selling skin cream. It is not creative, but I get free moisturiser and the extra income I need. Of course, I would love to go full-time freelance, or have an arts-related part-time job. Next year I am planning to go location independent for a while - I will freelance for a children's publishing company via Asia. Of course I will continue to be available for commissions too...

Why are blog giveaways such important promotion?
They give people a reason to visit and talk about your blog... and everybody loves the idea of a freebie! You can get yourself talked about, bring people to your blog, and connect directly with your readers - all of which can help to boost people's interest in your work, potentially resulting in future sales, commissions and a bit of buzz.

What do you sell on your Etsy store?
Precious Little Shop is only in its infancy but so far the pocket mirrors seem to be the most popular items. I think that the average person is more likely to buy merchandise than a print - not everyone has the time, space or inclination to hang a piece of art, but anyone can enjoy a decorated mirror, mug or t-shirt without having consciously to incorporate it into their lives. Etsy is saturated with hundreds-of-thousands of artists and their products,

so some kind of personal connection to potential buyers helps, whether it be real-world or through Twitter.

Where do you find the best blogs to follow?
I love following illustration and design blogs. Some of the best ones are Pikaland, Fuck Yeah Illustration! and Brown Paper Bag, but I also enjoy more personal ones such as those by Anna Emilia, Arts and Ghosts and Brett is a Blog. For fashion Dress a Day and LookBook are the places to go. I also cannot stress how much I love podcasts: Drawn Today, Ninja Mountain and Big Illustration Party Time inspire me to keep on going and entertain me as I work.

What are your views on ethical fashion?
Ethical fashion is definitely important to me. I enjoy clothes, style and fashion as much as anyone else, but I'm not a big fan of the industry itself. It is in a depressing state in terms of its treatment of workers and the disposable nature of clothing created for most High Street stores. It is obsessed with now, with youth, and with keeping itself in demand regardless of the consequences, which on some levels isn't healthy for consumers or the planet. Supporting and promoting talented ethical designers in places like Amelia's Magazine is an essential step towards persuading consumers to shop smarter and to be aware of the alternatives available, as well as making the world a better-dressed place.

How do your illustrations stand out from the crowd?
I am influenced by the 'golden age' of children's book illustration; I love the work of Rackham, Tenniel and Kay Nielsen. I also like the style of vintage girls' comics, and I think an interest in quirky details makes my work different from other fashion illustrators. I don't know of anyone whose working method is quite like mine, and believe that I have a unique style that doesn't look like anyone else's - hand-drawn and layered with details and textures, bringing together a vintage sensibility and modern fashions.

What's the best advice you can give an aspiring professional illustrator?
Work hard and create opportunities for yourself. Get a blog and or Twitter, do exhibitions, and connect with other people who are on the same wavelength. It never hurts to know your way around your computer because it makes you much more employable. It helps if you know how to get things print or web-ready, so teach yourself if you need to. Enjoy doing what you love! And don't do this if you don't love it, because it will never make you rich... unless you are very, very lucky.

Lu Flux A/W 2010, Dame & Knight

Erdem A/W 2010

Lu Flux A/W 2009, Old Believe

Lu Flux A/W 2010, Dame & Knight

ETHICAL FASHION DESIGNER: ORSOLA DE CASTRO

From Somewhere

You were one of the first fashion designers to embrace sustainability, way back in 1997. What prompted you to design in this way?

Back then it was not about the planet. It was about being original, creating one-offs and somehow maintaining a sense of humour - I loved putting rubbish into the best shops in the world. Eventually, as we progressed and realised how much was being dumped, both by the consumer and by the fashion and textile industry, it became an environmental issue - a design solution to an environmental problem.

How has the process of designing sustainably changed over the years?

When we discovered pre-consumer waste - offcuts, proofs, colour charts, damaged fabrics and end-of-line stock - design immediately became more challenging because we were no longer just customising anymore. It radically changed the quality of our garments and our capacity to fulfil bigger orders, thus reaching more shops, many internationally.

You have spoken of literally cleaning factory floors - do you turn up with a broom and just start sweeping?

Not quite brooms, but we do bring loads of boxes! We really do use the leftover material that no one else wants, thus providing a cleaning up service as we go along.

From Somewhere
Speedo collaboration S/S 2011

The factories, mills and manufacturers that we work with have adapted so well that sometimes they save stuff we haven't used before in a little trial box in case we might be interested in using it. More often than not we are. I think that it will be normal to have an in-house recycler very soon. Companies are starting to realise not just how much they waste, but also the creative potential of that waste. As well as the environmental benefits of reusing scraps there is a financial incentive too.

What is being thrown away?

Each scrap has a history that is often quite convoluted. Even though the recycling industry is now a fraction of what it was in places like Italy, a lot of textiles are still recycled quite extensively. Ends of rolls and scraps are sold in bulk to be used as insulation or similar, but even this type of recycling is wasteful of energy and water. We use the real waste that is destined to be landfilled or incinerated. The whole emphasis in the fashion industry has been on fast fast faster. Upcycling is a new term but of course it is not a new idea, it's just that in the past 25 years fast fashion has made the concept obsolete because it is more time consuming.

How do you ensure that you can produce your pieces in large numbers from reclaimed fabrics and end of line materials?

When we first started out we wanted to reach as many people as possible so we had to adapt to what buyers need - large quantities - while staying true to our cause. It is our speciality. After over ten years of designing in this way we now have a huge network of companies that are happy to give us their leftovers, and it is second nature for me to design in this way.

How did you get involved with the launch of Estethica?

We had been exhibitors at London Fashion Week since 2000, always selling very well, to well known stores. When the British Fashion Council decided they wanted an eco area they approached us to help out. They planned to put together a high-end exhibition and at that point we were the only eco brand that was also an exhibitor, vetted to the BFC's high standards. So Anna Orsini called us, and Estethica was born.

What other related projects are you involved in?

We consult quite a lot at the moment and I am also a speaker at all kinds of eco events. There is a big appetite for knowledge at the moment and we have the right experience to share, so we inevitably become involved in a multitude of other projects. We also really enjoy the process of collaboration, which is key.

For S/S 2011 you have collaborated with Speedo to produce a stunning range of glamorous dresses. How did this come about?

I am incredibly excited by the collection with Speedo because I adore the versatility of sportswear and high tech fabrics. It came about by word of mouth, as so often happens. Someone told us that Speedo had a lot of obsolete stock so we made a contact through a colleague and got hold of 5000 swimsuits. When Speedo saw what we had done with their dead stock they got very excited and it all snowballed from there. It is really hard to fault this kind of collaboration because it is such an easy way to be environmentally responsible. Speedo are way ahead of the game but many more companies will start to explore this concept. Of course, I am digging myself out of my own job here... but it's fun to spread the word.

J Smith Esquire S/S 2011

From Somewhere
Speedo collaboration S/S 2011

Tavi Gevinsson

From Somewhere
Speedo collaboration S/S 2011

Abigail Daker

self-portrait

Fine artist Abi Daker developed a love of fashion out of her studies of the human figure. Now residing in a tiny village half way up a mountain in Cyprus, she has rediscovered a love for the decorative aspect of fashion illustration. The sun shines for up to eight months a year and Abi often works outside - where bugs leave the occasional trail of footprints across her watercolour washes.

What is it that attracts you to fashion illustration?

When I first started an Fine Art degree, my main interest was in drawing the human figure. Life drawing wasn't encouraged on my course, so I needed to find other sources for my work. I started looking at fashion photography and adverts in magazines, then drawing from these images. I loved the dramatic exaggeration of the poses and outfits which often create surreal and interesting compositions. What I like most about fashion illustration is the scope it gives to make the images interesting and decorative. The majority of my professional work involves drawing subjects in a fairly literal way, but most of my personal work is quite abstract; fashion illustration is a great way to combine the two. I also love to work out a style and composition that reflects the aim of the fashion designer.

Why is ethical fashion important to you?

I'm concerned about a sustainable future; I have a child and I'd like the world to remain fairly stable for his future. We don't need fashion for day to day survival so we can easily make adjustments in the way we consume and it makes sense to encourage this. What I like about a lot of ethical fashion is that the designs are often quite classic and won't necessarily be outdated within weeks; if you can get someone to buy one coat every five years instead of three in a season then that's a good thing. I don't really like the throwaway fashion culture that places like Primark have encouraged; a lot of people are relentlessly buying clothes that they don't need and won't last because they are so cheaply made.

What is the process of creating your illustrations?

I always plot three lines down each side and divide the page up into nine boxes. This makes sure the image has a balanced structure and I can then loosen up a little once I'm working. I always draw the figure first then build up the shapes and patterns around it to reflect the movement of the figure and to balance the composition. The guide lines are often the main deciding factor in where I place any objects. I studied fine art under a really traditional, strict tutor so hand drawn and coloured images are pretty important to me. When I first started illustrating I spent a lot of time trying to create very bold, flat

areas of colour by hand but this is hard and there's usually some kind of break in the colour no matter how hard you try to keep it even. I found that it was much simpler to colour in digitally so now I scan the pen and ink drawings then even out the outlines and colour in the spaces on the computer.

How has living in Cyprus affected the way that you work?

Cyprus has a strong classical history but there are also a number of interesting contemporary artists around and in general the Cypriots have an excellent attitude to art. I've had a lot of commissions for a really wide range of projects and the landscape, the weather and the amazing light have really inspired me: though most of my commissioned work is done in the studio I frequently work outdoors as well.

How have social networks influenced your design process?

Social networks are a fantastic way of keeping up to date with creative news stories and events and they are a good way to talk to other artists. I've taken part in a few collaborative projects this year via Twitter which have made me consider new ways of working and different ways in which illustration can be applied.

Why is it important to keep developing your work?

On the last day of my degree course one of my tutors pointed out to me that I was just at the start of my artistic development and I've always tried to bear this in mind. Experimentation is important because there are so many different ways to create an illustration, and if I'm struggling to draw something then a different approach can often offer a great solution. I studied art because I love drawing, and constantly developing my work keeps me excited and interested in it. It's important for me to try new things: I never want to get jaded or bored by what I do.

What other kinds of illustration do you enjoy?

I love drawing city scenes, aerial landscapes, maps; landscape subjects are some of my favourite things to draw. My first illustrations were for children's books but over the past year I've started to feel that my work is probably best suited to older children; I've recently been working on illustrations for a fantasy novel, which I enjoyed a lot. I like to draw different subjects; it's interesting and means my work is constantly challenging.

And what do you do when you aren't drawing?

All my free time is spent with my little boy; swimming, taking him to the park or walking. The weather here is wonderful, so we're outdoors a lot.

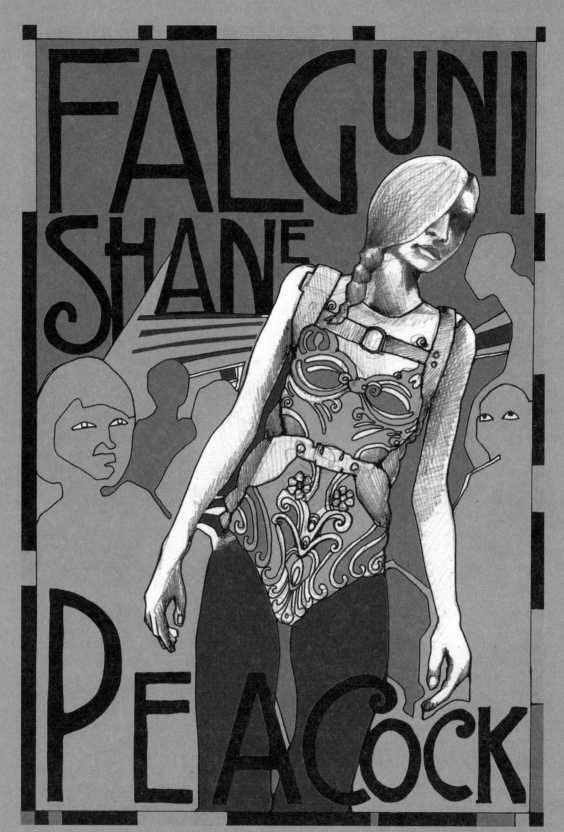

Falguni & Shane Peacock S/S 2011

es Saint Laurent

FAD Awards

Daks S/S 2011

Henrietta Ludgate

Scottish designer Henrietta Ludgate grew up in the wilds.

I grew up in the most idyllic environment for a child: my imagination ran wild in the woods, I collected frogs from the bog, and skated on the dark loch in winter. I aim to capture these vivid memories forever, in each collection. I'm inspired by Scottish folklore, the setting sun, the Northern Lights and the witching hour – the time when supernatural creatures are thought to be at their most powerful and magic is at its most effective. The Brahan Seer is a local mythical figure from the 17th century who was and still is renowned for his many prophecies which have continued to come true many generations after his tragic end.

Her trademark shape is a logo-less signature for those in the know.

I have developed a cylindrical trim that is an instantly recognisable trade mark for the cognoscenti, a discreet signature for those who are able to identify designer details, a subtle detail for the logo-phobic. I try to set the label apart with attention to detail, fine fabrics and exquisite workmanship that are the signal of slow fashion. Henrietta Ludgate clothing sets the wearer apart from the masses, symbolising a non-adherance to fast fashion, trendy logos and heavy branding.

Clothing as architectural art form.

My collections feature strong structural shapes to create a minimalist silhouette in luxurious British fabrics. A combination of sharp lines and drapes follow the contours of the body, meshing with Schiaparelli's view of clothing as a form of architecture that should be closely connected to the frame of the body, just as a building's form is drawn from its structural skeleton. I love the way that Elsa Schiaparelli regarded fashion as art, collaborating with artists

Henrietta Ludgate S/S 2011

such as Man Ray, Picasso, Salvador Dali and Alberto Gia-
cometti for an ultra modern outlook. Her constant innovation in design and fabric inspired my experimentation
process that has resulted in the architectural cylindrical
trim trade mark.

**An artisanal approach to design ensures traditional
quality and jobs for skilled locals.**

My highland background provides inspiration for design
and the best way of translating these ideas into reality
is by using materials found in that landscape. All materials are produced in and infused by the area and we
use organic materials where possible: to do anything
else would compromise both the design and ethos
of my collections. At the moment I really love
the luxury fabrics manufactured by Johnstons of
Elgin so I have their yarn cards and swatches
wallpapered around my studio. Their factory in the Highlands of Scotland is one of the
only fully integrated weaving plants in the UK
which means the spinning, weaving and dyeing are all done in one location using the very
latest in cutting edge technology. Johnstons
are world leaders in textile production, who
have worked with leading designers from
Hermes to Christopher Kane. However,
they still employ local skilled crafts-
men and women from start to finish in the manufacturing process, ensuring that skills
are preserved through
generations   of
families in the
Highlands.
I   have   also
worked   with
English company Lavenham Clothing, whose wonderful quilted fabrics have the almost magical ability to
stay cool in summer and warm in winter.

From design to finish, Henrietta makes perfect.

I start by creating a mood board of inspiration and
from this I develop the colour palette for the season,
then I create line drawings and experiment on the
stand with the first patterns and toiles. During this
time I also search for cloths, then we create the first
samples and revise them again and again until they
are perfect. This all takes place in-house; I am a very
hands-on designer and am involved in every aspect of
the manufacturing process.

Henrietta Ludgate A/W 2010

Sara Wadsworth at Graduate Fashion Week

ise Moody for Bobbin Bicycles

Katherine Tromans

Katherine Tromans is currently in her final year studying Illustration at the Arts University College at Bournemouth, but she is already proactively pursuing freelance editorial work because she wants to see her work published and in print. **I think it's important to have an idea of how freelance illustration works before I graduate.** Her degree is marked on how well she applies herself to the industry, so she is fully aware that anybody trying to get into the creative industry needs as much exposure as possible, by having a good website, entering competitions, and doing as much as possible before graduation. It may be hectic at college but a freelancer's life is extremely fast paced, a fact she learnt interning with Rob Ryan.

She recommends working for Amelia's Magazine as a great opportunity to see illustrations in context alongside an article. **It's exciting, fast-paced and definitely builds up your portfolio.** Katherine experiments with handmade techniques and different materials depending on the timescale of the brief. **I like to layer acetate and transparent paper, incorporating cut paper and paint as overlays.** She works instinctively and continuously pushes herself to explore new ways of creating illustrations.

For fashion illustration Katherine's favourite tools are different grades of pencil. **I love to draw on thick tracing paper with a good 2B pencil.** She starts with a notion of how the model might look by doing a few rough sketches, piecing together elements of the pose from various sources. **I then colour the image on a separate layer and scan these in.** Sometimes she uses a block of digital colour to create a background that will make the figure stand out. Fashion illustration is an integral part of the fashion design process: **I believe that an illustration can set a mood and add a personal touch that cannot easily be captured with photography.**

Fashion illustration can be quirky and beautiful because all illustrators see fashion designs from a different angle and they all have a different style. This makes it a great medium to raise awareness about green issues for people who would otherwise not know about ethical fashion.

As soon as Katherine got actively involved with Twitter, things started to happen. **I follow lots of creative people and there's always lots of competitions to get involved with.** She helped out with the Inkygoodness exhibition as a result of being on Twitter. **It's definitely a must have.**

self-portrait

Edun

Edun was launched by Ali Hewson and her rock star hubby Bono in 2005 to raise awareness of the possibilities for trade in Africa, with the proviso that all clothing is made with respect for the people who make the clothes, the place where they live and the materials used. Every factory along the supply chain is audited to ensure that everyone is treated fairly. In 2008 Edun established the Conservation Cotton Initiative in Uganda to support farmers with funding and training, and to ensure that they use sustainably produced cotton. In 2009 the fashion giant LVMH took a large stake in the business with the aim of growing responsible global trade, including the launch of collaborative designs between Edun and Louis Vuitton. New creative director Sharon Wauchob has spoken of her excitement about getting involved in the production side of the process. Because of the lack of infrastructure in Africa, Edun now manufactures more clothing in properly audited Chinese factories than it does in Africa. A small proportion of production still takes place in Africa, including the creation of beading and metal trim for garments, made in collaboration with the ethical jewellery company Made, who works with local artisans in Kenya.

Edun S/S 2011

Eugene Lin A/W 2010

Helen Taylor Graduate Collection 2010

Phoebe Coleman S/S 2011

Camilla Norrback

You've been involved in eco design since 2002. What prompted your decision to make your label sustainable?

It was an easy choice, considering the world we live in and all the changes we need to make in order to keep our planet alive. Of course it's no quick fix and all the things that need to be done are overwhelming – but we need to start somewhere. That's my philosophy. Everybody needs to try and do something, however small, and then we can make big changes happen. It makes my job more meaningful if I can contribute to these changes, and being 'eco' has more to do with how I run my company than it has to do with my design.

What does sustainability mean to you?

To make sustainable clothes it is important to consider the whole production of a garment, from idea to finished product. As well as using organic fabrics I also concentrate on how the materials are grown, transported, coloured and sewn. I also make sure that we keep a close long-term relationship with our suppliers and of course that the styles I make last for several seasons, both in fashion and in quality.

What is Ecoluxury?

Ecoluxury is the modern luxury, a high-fashion garment that is produced fairly and ecologically. It adds a new dimension to the clothing, and the wearer can feel both beautiful and proud. I think it's something that all companies can aspire to, whether they make cars, buildings or clothes. The fact is that in the very near future we won't be able to think in any other way. The survival of our planet will depend on whether or not we can adjust our production and consumption to become sustainable. Quality will become more and more important because we won't be able to consume in the same quantities in the future. The problem will solve itself.

What changes have you noticed in the industry?

When I started there was hardly anything apart from organic cotton on the market, but now new materials are being introduced all the time, and you can find fibres in everything from soya bean to milk. Soybean fibre is often referred to as vegetable cashmere because it is so soft and its amino acids are also healthy for your skin. It is made out of leftover materials from tofu and soya milk production and as well as being biodegradable no fertilisers, pesticides or herbicides are used in its production. More and more companies have realised that costumers are looking for ecological products on a larger scale than before, so they are able to profit from being sustainable. Things are heading in the right direction but of course there's still more to do.

What are your influences?

I always look back in time before starting up a new collection. I get inspired by the shapes, colours and details of garments from yesterday, and all my designs hint at my love of nostalgic and retro-romantic styles. I love the dark and mournful Paris of the 1920's, and I'm a big fan of old Hitchcock films as well as 80's teen movies. A mixture of influences really. I aim for a combination of functionality and femininity when I design.

What is the inspiration for your S/S 2011 collection?

My latest collection is inspired by my memories of childhood summers in Swedish Finland. I drew inspiration from the historic Carlsro house, which from the 1890's has been the scene of both blessed socialite lifestyles and tragic fates. I looked at the architecture, the mystic atmosphere, the beautiful patterns on the tiles, the lace tablecloths, secret passageways, faded colours, shadows and past feelings. The garments are made from soft cotton jersey, twill, fine cotton, lace knits and lace fabrics. I have also used recycled materials such as lace made out of recycled polyester. Shoes are made of natural tanned leather, cork and recycled rubber.

Camilla Norrback A/W 2010

Penelope Trappes of The Golden Filter

Jennifer Costello

FASHION ILLUSTRATOR

Jenny Costello is proud to hail from the traditional centre of textile manufacturing in the UK, and since finishing her degree in Illustration at the Birmingham Institute of Art and Design she has since moved back to her home town of Sutton Coldfield in the Midlands.

Jenny is passionate about illustration as a form of communication. Her figures tend to be simple and true to life, but she goes to town on the garments themselves, creating artwork on cardboard, recycled materials or plywood. Watercolour is absorbed by the wood, creating a wonderfully forgiving translucent organic aesthetic. Of course the trouble is that painting on plywood incurs extra costs and storage issues, but creating an illustration on a plain piece of white paper is intimidating by comparison. Feminine designs are instinctive to Jenny, who is one of four sisters.

Jenny is like a magpie, always after glitter and intricacies. She adds detail to encourage the viewer to spend more time observing her illustrations: "In fact I think I'm just greedy," she says. "I crave visual stimulation, and I indulge in a bit of escapism when there's loads of detail, colour and texture." She is inspired by florals, foliage, anything natural and organic - because the patterns in nature are amongst the most seductive. Intricate textiles such as knitwear are especially enticing because of their detail and Pia Anjou's clean unfussy tailoring paired with ditsy patterned fabrics is an aesthetic that fits perfectly with her illustrative style. In fact, Pia Anjou creates clothing that Jenny would wear herself.

During the evenings Jenny scours her favourite publications, online blogs and websites for ideas, inspiration and opportunities. Creating illustrations for Amelia's Magazine has been good for seeking constructive criticism and developing concepts quickly, and she has just landed a job with a well known greetings card company thanks in part to her work for the magazine. "The studio manager collected Amelia's Magazine (in print). She's a big fan."

self-portrait v

Partimi

ETHICAL FASHION DESIGNER:
ELEANOR DORRIEN-SMITH

Your current collection was inspired by the dresses of Diaghilev's Ballet Russes that your grandmother bought at auction in Sothebys. She sounds like a very inspirational character. What kind of woman is your grandmother?

My grandmother loves collecting things and her attention has turned to some interesting areas including 18th and 19th century farming equipment, all things cowboy and Western... and the Ballet Russes. I have certainly inherited the pack-rat tendency and I have visions of myself in later life sitting surrounded by a lifetime's worth of hoarding! Over time many of my grandmother's collections have been sold on but I still love to visit and wade my way through cabinets and cupboards to see what treasures she still has.

How do you give the impression of 'hurried repairs' in this collection?

The hurried repairs I found the most interesting were the haphazard darning attempts that conjure up visions of seamstresses sitting in the wings of the stage desperately trying to repair costumes. The darning effect was explored in a knit dress I designed with Central Saint Martins graduate Hiroko Nakajima, where we imitated the effect of loose threads within the knit and then worked into the areas by hand using loose darning techniques. I also love all the hand-painted decoration that has been repainted over and over again, leaving areas all cracked and textured over time. To express this I layered multiple monoprints to create a subtle yet rich texture.

You won a prize at the Fashioning the Future Awards in 2009. How has this helped you to gain recognition?

Winning this prize was a wonderful opportunity to have my work shown to a panel of leaders in both the ethical and fashion industries. It also gave me the chance to show a preview collection with the Centre for Sustainable Fashion on their stand at Estethica during London Fashion Week. This experience allowed me to meet buyers and press, measure their reactions to my work and plan how I was going to move forward for the following season.

How do the t-shirts fit into your collection?

My t-shirts started as a project to complement a collection I created for S/S 2010 which was inspired by the problems of overfishing. They soon became pretty popular and with their combination of simple, graphic and sometimes tongue-in-cheek designs they served as a great way to get the message out about overfishing and to gain recognition for PARTIMI. I then created two more designs for the Environmental Justice Foundation in reaction to the 2010 Gulf of Mexico oil spill. Recently my attention has been taken up by my ready-to-wear collection but soon the two projects will come together.

The photos of your new collection are really beautiful.

What inspired the feel of the shoot?

Sepia photographs of the dancers and artists in Diaghilev's company relaxing in beautiful wild gardens and old houses and dreamy images of my grandmother in the late 60's and 70's. The photographer Nicole Maria Winkler really understood the effect I wanted and the results are stunning.

How did your collaboration with Joanna Cave come about and what was the process of working together?

I met Joanna at the A/W 2010 Estethica exhibition at London Fashion Week. I had already started on the designs for my next collection and I felt that Joanna's delicate style would be perfect for capturing some of the details on the costumes. When Joanna was in London we sat in a cafe and worked through inspiration and ideas, then we sent each other sketches and samples, each editing the results down to our favourites. Joanna created some samples in silver and we made our final decisions based on these. We then each designed our own pieces and Joanna finished them up in her studio in Greece.

What are your plans for the future?

Collaborative designs are a strength of my current collection and as I develop the identity of PARTIMI I plan to continue working with experienced and graduate designers to make collaboration an inherent part of the brand. My long-term goal is to have a collection of studios and retail environments selling both PARTIMI and visiting designers.

PARTIMI 2008 That Far Away Place

Pia Anjou

Mixing cute florals with masculine tailoring, the Pia Anjou design aesthetic has recently toured the world as part of the Swedish Institute Eco Chic exhibition.

We all need to slow down.

Pia Anjou loves vintage styles, old portrait photos and the feel of old film. Her website features beautiful pictures taken on a Holga film camera and an ancient Lubitel that once belonged to her mother. Whenever she needs new inspiration she takes photos that open her eyes to a new world of colours and compositions.

A third generation tailor.

Both her grandmother and her mother were dressmakers so it made perfect sense for Pia to study knitwear at the renowned Swedish School of Textiles in Boras. Pia embraced sustainability because there is no alternative.

"We must all stop and think: the fashion industry is dirty enough."

Collaborating with other artists.

The musician Jenny Wilson wore some of her clothes for an interview so Pia contacted her to see if she wanted some more, which of course she did. She thinks it is important to support good artists who have the same outlook on the world.

Owning a store.

The Pia Anjou label is sold in her Gothenburg shop, mixed in with vintage clothes from the 1950's and earlier, as well as some homeware and furniture. She takes on a few freelance jobs to help out her business but she hopes in the near future to spend more time experimenting with her own designs.

Pia Anjou S/S 2010

Pia Anjou S/S 2010

Charlie Boots S/S 2010

Ethical Beauty

Gemma Milly

Long term Amelia's Magazine contributor Gemma Milly started off in advertising before making the decision to change her career drastically and take up an MA in illustration. Once she'd decided to pursue her lifelong love of drawing she called an ex course tutor for advice on what to put in a portfolio and promptly got a place on the MA in Illustration at Kingston University. Since then Gemma has produced numerous illustrations for Amelia's Magazine that have served as encouragement in what can sometimes be quite a lonely profession, as well as attracting lots of interest from creatives. She regards fashion illustration as akin to the job of a stylist, communicating ideas through imagery.

self-portrait

What made you give up a glamorous career in advertising?
My first degree was in Management & French and after graduation I moved straight into advertising where I spent a wonderful few years working on fabulous accounts with a great team. I was quite happily climbing the career ladder whilst enjoying the perks of working in the industry... until I started work at a certain design agency. My boss and I clashed so badly that she made me reappraise what I wanted out of life and I realised that I didn't want to be a 'suit' anymore. I decided that my passion lay in illustration so I left behind my life of working lunches and cabs to become a student again.

How has studying for a Masters in Illustration helped you to develop your style and your plans for your career?
When I began my MA I felt as if I'd well and truly stepped out of my comfort zone. I'd gone from being able to do my job standing on my head to being the new girl and it was initially quite daunting. A lot of people on the course had come from graphic design backgrounds and had more creative experience than me. I also worried about having a style, but as time passed I realised that I loved the challenge of answering creative briefs and that the way I drew was becoming more coherent. The beauty of an MA is that you shape your own briefs, so it allowed me to concentrate on the areas of illustration that interested me the most and by the end I knew that I wanted to specialise in fashion illustration. Luckily, having worked previously in advertising and design I have met many wonderful people which will hopefully prove useful as contacts in my future career.

What does your studio space look like?
It's not the most glamorous space! I have a big old table that is usually covered in paper, fine-liners, watercolours and piles of magazines. I need a constant supply of apples, coffee and good music to keep me going. Depending on my mood, this could be anything from Wax Tailor or Ed Solo to Oceansize or Tool. Then I'm set for the day. Mostly, I like to create my illustrations using pencil and/or fineliner on cartridge paper. I then add colour by creating washes on watercolour paper, sometimes using masking fluid, salt crystals or mixing with gouache to create different effects, before combining it all in Photoshop.

Jessica Thompson Graduate Collection 2010

Jacob Kimmie A/W 2010

Swishing

Carlotta Gherzi
for Sado A/W 2010

Caroline Charles A/W 2010

Victor Chan Graduate Collection 2010

Why do you enjoy creating images through traditional methods before digitally enhancing them?

I love paint and pencils so I would never give these up in favour of a Mac. I have a great appreciation for artists who create their images entirely using a computer, but I love the unpredictability of traditional materials and the hand-made finish you can achieve. Saying that, I would definitely not be without my Mac or my Wacom! If you know how to use these tools properly, they can be invaluable in enhancing your work and making it look professional. I mainly use the Mac to layer colour, texture and pattern in my images and I think it gives my images a more polished feel than I could achieve with traditional methods alone.

Why do you find so much inspiration in fashion?

Fashion runs so much deeper than just an aesthetic. We use it as a form of self-expression, it can alter our mood and shape our identity, and this aspect is exactly what I love to capture in my illustrations. I am also a firm believer that fashion and art are intrinsically linked and that they both enrich our lives through their diversity. If you look at a garment as a piece of art, and imagine what the designer is trying to communicate, you can't help but be inspired. Historically there has always been a love affair between art and fashion, from the Renaissance, when painters first tried to capture the form, colour, and texture of clothing, to today, when models strut down the runway in virtual works of art. You only have to look at the Dada-inspired hats of Schiaparelli and armadillo shoes of Alexander McQueen to see this. Without fashion, our lives would be much less colourful.

Can you tell us more about your character Agent Amandine?

Agent Amandine is a character that I developed for a spoof glossy magazine of the same name, as part of my MA final major project. The plot goes something like this: girl works in advertising, girl gets sick of her job, accidentally gets tangled up in an undercover plot to investigate crimes against fashion and so begins a double life. It's meant to be a light-hearted take on the graphic novel, but aimed at young females. Amandine is a character that I think a lot of women who work in media will relate to, and whose escapades will bring a wry smile to their faces! You could say that the story is slightly autobiographical and although it's quite tongue in cheek in parts, I do think the underlying plot is a pretty fair representation of a lot of twenty-somethings' lives in London.

Why is it so important to create pretty images to look at, especially in the field of ethical fashion design?

I sometimes worry that I'm not making some profound statement with my illustrations, but my aim is to create something beautiful and engaging, and a little eye candy never went amiss. People contact me on my blog and Twitter to say how much they love my illustrations, so I must be doing something right. I think sometimes the perception of ethical fashion is that it's drab, so if I can create striking, eye-catching images and use the medium to raise awareness about fairtrade, organic materials and sustainable fashion practices, then that's no bad thing.

In an ideal world where would you illustrate from and what would your ideal work space look like?

That's easy, I'm a total Francophile so if I could illustrate from anywhere in the world it would be Paris. I spent a year there in my early twenties and fell in love with the city. For inspiration in every shape and form it's a wonderful place to be, and the culture is so rich that I would never run out of things to draw. I'm also definitely a people person, so my perfect workspace would be a bright, sunny loft-style studio in Montmartre shared with a couple of other creatives. This dream studio would have a little park nearby for baguette munching, a wonderful Amelie-style café next door for coffee drinking/macaroon gobbling and a nice selection of shoe shops for credit card abusing.

What are the most important things to lead a fulfilled life?

The things that make me happy in life are a job I love, a full social life and fabulous friends and family. Oh, and enough money to fund my shoe addiction. If was offered my old job on a plate along with the perks and salary, in exchange for being a struggling artist just starting out, I wouldn't take it. Although it's nice to be able to buy whatever I want and not worry about it, you can't put a price on being happy. I love that I can wake up and plan my day exactly how I want to, doing something that gets me genuinely excited. I still have a great social life and am able to travel with my work as I'm not tied down to an office job. That said, the profession of an illustrator can often be a lonely one, so I ensure I make the most of social networking with Facebook, Twitter, LinkedIn and lots of blogging. I can't stress enough how important it is to get your work out there when you're just starting out, and to make as many connections and contacts as you can. You never know when someone you've chatted to might give you your next break. Talking to people 'virtually' also stops me going insane when I've spent all day on my own, slaving over a pencil and sketchbook.

Bora Aksu A/W 2010

Ari Up RIP 1962-2010

Zara Gorman MA Graduate Collection 2010

Minna S/S 2011

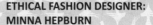

How has the way you create your clothes progressed since you first started out?

I think fashion should be fun; I just love to put on a dress which brings a smile to my face. We have kept our feminine, vintage inspired, playful style but the collection is a bit more grown up, which has helped us to find a new audience. Lace still plays a big part in the collection but we have also started to use heavier fabrics such as wool jersey. I prefer to keep our colourways simple but we are designing a print to use for linings and dresses in our next collection. The recession has also played a role in our design process - we have had to think about our price points and make sure that our pieces are multi-functional. We still focus on UK-made fabrics and all production is based in London, since this is integral to the brand.

Where do you source your fabrics from?

Sourcing fabrics is a big part of the job so we do a lot of networking. I am lucky to have designer friends who are happy to share information about their suppliers, and sourcing fabrics online has improved massively over the last two years, but I still find it very difficult to source UK-made fabrics: we desperately need a good supplier database. Sourcing vintage lace is a fun part of the job because I love strolling around antique markets. Unfortunately I have very little time to do that these days so I go on Ebay instead and when travelling I can't resist visiting the local antique fairs. Lace can be very expensive if you go to proper antique shops so I rely on local grannies who know where to buy it in bulk.

How do you ensure a commercial collection?

We buy Scottish lace in massive quantities and mix it with other fabrics, but we don't produce entire one-off pieces because these would be tricky to sell online. However, because most of our pieces are embellished with offcuts and antique lace they are unique. This is very labour intensive so the price has to reflect that.

Can you describe how each piece is made, from conception to finish?

We always work from the fabrics first, and then we try to incorporate popular styles that have already sold well, changing the cut slightly. I look for ideas everywhere and I particularly love blogs and websites that display street styles from all over the world. We do all sampling, designing and embellishing in-house and production is then based all over London. Controlling production and quality takes up the majority of my time because it is so labour intensive.

How did you come to be based in London?

I live in London these days but part of me still belongs to Dorset. It was such a peaceful place for my kids to grow up and the pace of life was perfect, but the business would never have taken off in Dorset because it was impossible to find skilled artisans. I love the creative energy in London and there are so many talented people to work with. I grew up in Finland and moved to the UK over a decade ago but of course Finland will always have a special place in my heart; fortunately I get to visit regularly because our business is doing very well there.

You first label SE1 London was manufactured in Vietnam. Why did you decide to change direction and embrace ethical design?

Vietnam is such a gorgeous place and I felt privileged to work with very strong and kind women who took good care of their employees. The working conditions were better than I have seen in some factories here; the cafeteria served breakfast and a hot meal to the workers every day. I have nothing but good impressions about manufacturing in Vietnam and I would do it again in a heartbeat. It was because of the way that the UK fashion industry operates at the High Street level that I decided to turn my back on fast fashion.

What is your favourite garment to wear out of your own collections?

I love my A/W 2011 collection. We put a lot of thought into that collection and each piece is so wearable, sometimes in different ways. For example the Ira dress has an amazing detachable bird necklace made from recycled leather and antique watch parts. Claudia is a very grownup piece, Dorothy is a great party dress and I love the pockets on the Tia dress. I used to love designing the summer collections but these days winter would my favourite season. There are so many amazing wool suppliers in the UK that I will never run out of ideas.

What best describes Eco Luxe?

For me it is all about luxurious, good quality fabrics with fabulous cut, attention to detail and finishing. We do everything possible to minimise our impact on the environment.

Christopher Raeburn

ETHICAL FASHION DESIGNER

Christopher Raeburn studied at Middlesex University in London, where a really good technical tutor made him keen to attend the hallowed Royal College of Art, from which he graduated in 2006. He has become well known for his upcycling of military fabrics, although he has worked with everything from Eurostar uniforms to hot air balloon material. He sources parachutes, leather jackets, tents and ponchos from military surplus warehouses around England, but has increasingly started to import pieces from Europe so that he can make bigger runs. The military inherently overproduces so there are huge volumes of fabric and garments that will never be used - dead stock that Christopher is happy to make the most of. In fact most production processes are inefficient so there is always likely to be pre-consumer waste; for example, 10% of the parachute fabric that is made fails opacity tests. Christopher is able to give that fabric a new lease of life. Most recently he worked with windproof cotton from some forty year old Swedish snow parkas. Occasionally a company will contact him about a specific material they think he might like to use, which has been a great way to keep his collections fresh and innovative.

Remade in England garments are limited edition, so named because Christopher is proud to be a British designer: "It gives me an obligation to be thoughtful, innovative and a bit playful with the design process." These pieces are deconstructed and remade in-house. Fabric offcuts are used to create collectible woodland creatures and accessories. Christopher recently collaborated with menswear designer Tim Soar, which gave his garments exposure on the catwalk at London Fashion Week and helped to raise interest in his own label. He works with a tight team to create a strong image for the Christopher Raeburn brand and this season he was the first designer to move from Esthetica into NEWGEN, successfully straddling the worlds of mainstream and ethical fashion. Christopher believes the best way to promote sustainable fashion is to make great design that changes perceptions and his brand is the perfect example of how to build a sustainable worldwide business with a valid voice within mainstream fashion. He also teaches a menswear module at Nottingham Trent University where he hopes to influence a new generation of designers.

Christopher Raeburn A/W 2010

Jo Cheung

FASHION ILLUSTRATOR

Creating a mess.

I like to be hands-on with with my work because I want to be connected with the whole process of production. I start with hand drawn images and collages in my sketchbook then I scan them into my computer. I produce much better work when I make a bit of a mess - images fully constructed in Photoshop never look as good. Of course I use the computer to retouch my images but I don't do super, super slick.

Music and piles of paper.

I have piles of paper, glue and stickers kicking about everywhere. Generally it looks as though I've demolished my studio! I'll start work on my desk then spread out onto the floor and coffee table; there's never enough room for me. I call it creative mess... and I have to listen to music; I really can't work in silence. Usually ambient, electronica or dubstep gets me in the mood but I'm always on the lookout for interesting new bands.

self-portrait

Finding a style.

I had a really good time during my foundation year in college because we were given so much freedom to do our own thing; great tutors are always a bonus. Through trial and error I found my strength was in making collages, often using my huge collection of stickers, most of of which I've had for ten years. I love to incorporate anything brightly coloured, kitsch and plastic into my illustrations. I get most of my references for fashion illustrations from my huge collection of magazines which I never throw away.

A whimsical rural idyll.

I often prefer to create an imaginary world rather than draw from reality. My new personal work is called Landscape and Dreams, based on the idea of a whimsical world far away from the banality of daily life. I created a fantasy world for the Landscape issue of Blanket Magazine, based on my childhood memories of living amongst the paddy fields and hills in rural Hong Kong. I tend to reminisce and daydream a lot.

Having fun with fashion.

I have a lot of respect for innovative designers like Galliano, Alexander McQueen, Dior and Eley Kishimoto. I once aspired to be a fashion designer but I just don't have the patience. Instead I like to reflect the fun elements of fashion collections in my illustrations.

Teaching brings rewards.

After I left college I decided to apply for some community work because I like meeting new people. Now I work part time with autistic children, and I love it; we do a lot of creative craft sessions. I would get bored if I did the same thing every day and because I run sessions on my own it has taught me to multi-task very well. I am very happy to come home and work on illustrations till midnight.

A Yorkshire childhood.

My home town of Doncaster is not exactly the land of dreams: pound shops, boy racers, run down 60's buildings... the lack of creative opportunities spurred me on to work really hard and get into university in London. If I'd stayed there I'm pretty sure I wouldn't be where I am now. But of course I'm proud to be northern.

The power of Twitter.

Twitter keeps me updated about what other artists are up to and I love to meet up with Twitter friends in real life. I get a lot of traffic to Etsy, Society6 and Facebook via links on Twitter. Basically, you will find me everywhere on the internet. Twitter is a great way to stay connected, but I tend to dip in and out to promote my work and give shout outs to other artists because otherwise I get too distracted when I am working.

Leila Hafzi S/S 2009, UTOPIA

Hermione de Paula A/W 2010

Leila Hafzi S/S 2009
UTOPIA

Ciel S/S 2011

Ciel

Sarah Ratty of Ciel was one of the first designers to engage in ethical practice in the UK. She set up the label Conscious Earthwear in the early 90's before creating the Ciel brand in 2005. She currently also works as a design consultant and advises the Soil Association on sustainable issues.

How do you design your garments?

Each collection has its roots in the way I have developed as an eco fashion designer over the last twenty years. I usually start with fabrics, then I think about what garment shapes will best fit into the current zeitgeist and I combine these with my own influences from contemporary art, travel, history and nature. I use as many innovative approaches as I can in fabrication and cutting techniques, as well as using the naturally diverse fabrics from a range of indigenous locations, which are made and developed in situ.

What is the best way to design ethically?

Within eco design there is inevitably some compromise but I always do my best to find the best materials to achieve the desired outcome. I use fairtrade materials and organic fabrics from factories in Europe and South America, all of which comply with fair labour laws as set out by Labour Behind the Label. We use azo-free dyes, which do not use harmful metal mordants to fix the colour. Heavy metals are highly polluting and contribute to toxic soil runoff if not treated correctly. We have

recently started to bring some production back to the UK and we conduct a lot of our work via Skype to reduce our carbon footprint.

Is there a lot of competition between ethical designers?

I think that most fashion designers are sympathetic to each other because each one has a unique approach. I believe that, as in nature, there is plenty of room for everyone to create what they need to do, and I am currently collaborating with some complementary high street brands to enable our product to reach a wider market place: a win win situation for all concerned.

Do we have any modern day ethical icons now that Anita Roddick is no longer here?

I guess that Katharine Hamnett has taken up the role that Anita left behind, and has done some great pioneering work within the fashion industry through the Environmental Justice Foundation and working with farmers in the field via the Pesticide Action Network.

Which country is leading the way when it comes to ethical and sustainable fashion?

Many countries are now actively developing their green textile supply chains, including China, which is the natural home for the majority of hemp production. Each country has its specialist fibre production, for instance in the UK it is wool, in Peru it's Alpaca, in Africa, Egypt, India and parts of South America it's different types of cotton, and Europe as a whole is known for its textile innovation.

Eun Jeong S/S 2011

Antipodium S/S 2011

Antipodium S/S 2011

Faye West

Illustrator Faye West has been fascinated by the human figure in clothing for as long as she can remember. After studying fashion illustration in London she returned to Devon, where she now creates her illustrations with pencil, watercolour and her trusty scanner.

Why is illustration as a whole so important to you?

I get so much enjoyment from the outcome of a quick creative flourish that I can't wait to scan my artwork and see it finished, which sometimes makes me quite impatient. I don't feel articulate when it comes to expressing ideas in writing, so using images as a narrative is much easier for me. Certain favourite children's book illustrations have stayed with me forever and I can only hope to leave something as influential behind.

How do you get from "princess and dancing girls" to the catwalk?

For pure escapism I used to draw the outfits from Hollywood musicals and romantic films such as The Red Shoes, always inspired by the relationship between the clothes and the body. I loved the styling details; leg of mutton sleeves, pinafores and petticoats, bodices and trains. I became obsessed by costume, criticising any film that hadn't researched their dates correctly... but I also became intrigued by each era's idiosyncratic portrayal of historic costume. For example the Greek or Roman ladies in the epic bible story films of the 50's and 60's managed also to portray the fashions of the time in such a fun way. There are bullet bras on the heroines in Westerns, and films from the 70's had such fun recreating the fashions of the 20's and 30's.

How do you create a fashion illustration?

I create the image in pencil from a photograph or screen image, and as soon as the proportions are right I can't wait to use watercolours. Quite often the features will be of someone entirely different whose looks interested me at another time. Sometimes I colour in the pencil image on Photoshop and create a kaleidoscopic repeat design with it. I discovered Spoonflower purely by chance when a fellow Twitterer recommended them for customised printing on organic fabrics. I have just ordered my first roll of fabric and I hope that my dear mum will help me produce some cosmetic and shopping bags to sell. I would also love to produce stationary. Every gift shop in Devon stocks Cath Kidston and I would like to get a look in.

You delivered cupcakes to me years ago, which made me very happy - why did you decide to make such a sweet and unique gesture, and then never follow it up?
I applied for the only course in the UK that I could find

self-portrait

Patrick Wolf

Comme de Garçons

Minna S/S 2011

Andrea Crews A/W 2010

which specifically taught fashion illustration but unfortunately it didn't quite deliver the focus on illustration the title of the course had led me to believe. Everyone else decided to take up styling, photography or marketing when they graduated, so I was left without a community of illustrators to bounce around ideas of how to establish myself. And to be honest, my course wasn't very helpful in any practical aspect of how to obtain work, paid or unpaid. I came up with the idea of illustrated cupcakes when I was living with friends from the London College of Fashion and they were a real labour of love; unfortunately I didn't quite understand that I needed to follow up my gesture and look for illustration call outs to promote my work further. Thanks to being on Twitter I am now better placed to get my work out there!

You made a big move down to Devon a few years ago - how has this impacted your illustration work?

I lived on Lundy Island ten miles off the Devonshire coast for a year as a result of looking for a job that didn't entail yet more shop work. It's three miles long and has one shop, one pub and a population of around 25. It was a marvellous and unique transition from London life to being back in Devon, where I grew up. There isn't much to do apart from walking, dry stone walling or tree planting, so it was the perfect chance to really immerse myself in fine art and I barely did any fashion artwork during this time because I was so busy working on large scale pieces in pen and ink... working with an old fashioned medium on an island that time forgot. The break did me good in the long run because I was refreshed and enthusiastic when I came back to settle in North Devon; ready to focus on fashion and music artwork again.

What do you miss about London?

There are so many things I don't miss about trying to get by in London; I had no time to get on with anything creative because I spent so much time travelling around and by the time I got home I was always so tired that I had no energy to draw. But I miss being able to go to the cinema or visit a gallery by myself without anyone thinking anything of it. I miss the exciting smell of any given evening, knowing that so many events are happening all over the city. I miss my friends and the diversity of characters and backgrounds of the colleagues I used to work with. And of course I miss the fashion.

How has getting an agent helped your career?

I spent the first few years out of college sending work to agencies and failing to get any work published or used, which knocked my confidence in my abilities. So finding Restless Artists was a godsend. I joined the agency just before I left London and it gave me an enormous confidence boost, otherwise I would have felt as if I was returning to Devon with my tail between my legs. Restless Artists is currently helping me to plan an exhibition.

What fine art projects are you working on?

My Six States of Intoxication started when I was bored at work one evening and decided to wikipedia what happens to the human body in a state of drunkenness. There are six states, including Euphoria, Coma and Death, so I decided to work on some Hogarth type pieces. Each of the six pieces profiles a notorious London alcoholic from history, their story matching one of the states. Strangely the only living person (representing our present time) was artist Sebastian Horsley, who emailed me an anecdote to use, just shortly before his death following a drug binge.

Why has social networking become so important to you?

I'm not surrounded by artists, writers or fashion people anymore and therefore the only information I can gather these days is via the internet or publications. Twitter is amazing; sometimes I hear about exhibitions and other cultural news even before my London friends do, so it has become a vital life line for me as a rural based illustrator. I wish I had joined earlier. The internet is my main window into everything creative and inspirational, and I couldn't cope without it. There is so much talent to discover online that never makes it into mainstream publications and it's incredible just how many visitors visit my blog from far away lands.

How should ethical fashion be made more widely available?

I wish, like being female in the music business, that ethical fashion wasn't a separate genre. All the high street chains seem to sell the same mass produced tat that has been shipped over from Asia: what we need are lots of independent shops that are willing to source desirable ethical fashion from local emerging designers.

Has anything good happened as a result of working with Amelia's Magazine?

To be honest I've received more guidance in my career from working with Amelia's Magazine than I ever did at university. Taking part in open briefs has helped me to develop so much as an illustrator, and even more excitingly I've just been asked to create some print designs for an ethical fashion designer as a result of all the work I've been doing with Amelia's Magazine.

Minna

Oria S/S 2011

Gossypium

Gossypium worked with Amelia's Magazine and Brie Harrison to create a Clothkits-inspired kit fashion dress and bag to accompany the final print issue of Amelia's Magazine. Run by Abigail and Thomas Petit, it is a family business based in Lewes, East Sussex.

What is your process of creating your garments?

We do things the opposite way around to the rest of the fashion industry. I was working as a textile engineer with Indian farmers when we started Gossypium, so fabric comes first: from the spinning of the yarn to the final stitching of the garments is a long and complicated process. We have an extremely close working relationship with our producers and a huge respect for their hard work and care of the environment.

Why is transparency more important than certification?

In some instances enforced standards have some value, for example it is good to be able to label something organic or fairtrade, but sometimes the point of certification gets clouded and this can limit good honest business practice. Transparency and brand trust are the most precious and valuable assets. Knowing our trade and suppliers so well shows in the quality of our products, and this benefits our customers. And it means that no one can copy us or take those relationships away.

Why did you decide to collaborate with Amelia's Magazine and Brie Harrison?

We are pioneers who have built our entire business from scratch so it was lovely to concentrate on something that was more fashion-based for a change. Working with Amelia's Magazine allowed us to have a fantastic burst of creativity and we sure enjoyed that moment. Nula Shearing, who is a daughter of the Clothkits family, has just created a lovely tea towel for us, and we hope to do more fashion-led designs in the future.

In what other ways do you live an ethical life?

The company is growing much more slowly than it could do because we spend a lot of time together as a family. Everyone gets involved: our teenagers are the best sales girls we've ever had and our six year old knows how to check the change from a fiver. Even our four year old knows just how many sweets she can get for a modelling shoot. Our ethic is to think global act local, and that starts at home with homemade dinners together every night.

What are your latest plans for the label?

We are about to add a 'fashion bar' to our Lewes shop, where customers will become designers, adding their own choice of vintage bows and buttons to otherwise plainish items.

Erica Sharp

FASHION ILLUSTRATOR

Erica Sharp is passionate about her twin roles as illustrator and arts educator. Her work utilises to great effect the traditional Japanese paper cutting techniques that come so naturally to her.

How and why were you taught to fold origami?

I was very young when my Japanese mother and grandmother taught me traditional origami, an art form used to express the Japanese love and respect for nature. One of my first memories is of a giant decorative ball of origami made by my great grandmother to hang inside our house in Japan. A few years ago I returned to live in Japan in a town famous for making decorative Washi paper and I became fascinated with the detail of Kiri-e paper cut art. Kiri-e artwork can be minimal or extremely intricate and is also used in other countries including China and Poland. It felt right to experiment with Washi paper and Kiri-e techniques to create lovely hand cut illustrations, a process I have been working with ever since.

How do you work with Japanese washi paper?

I think about what personalities my girls might have as I sketch out rough poses in pencil. Once I am happy with my composition I go over the drawing in pen, leaving space for the areas I want to embellish with paper. I try to think about the structure of the clothing and how it is pieced together so that I can emulate this with the shapes and layers of Washi paper that I cut or tear to arrange and then stick down to complete the illustration. I am also experimenting with ways to combine brightly cut paper and black and white photography.

Why do you enjoy creating fashion illustrations?

I love fashion because it is all about fantasy and masquerade, and I think all women enjoy playing with their identity. Fashion photography is really inspiring but fashion illustration allows me to really explore and experiment with the subtle magic of fashion. I also love seeing how other illustrators bring fashion designs to life.

What drew you to the work of ethical designer Satoshi Date?

Less is more and his designs are elegant and feminine in their simplicity. The imperfections of his hand-dyed organic materials and the intricate embroidery of his accessories bring an interesting quality to his work which is reminiscent of traditional Japanese craft techniques and the translucency of some of his materials reminded me of paper, so they were perfect to illustrate.

Why is it important for you to draw ethical fashion?

It's really exciting to be able to make ethical fashion attractive through my illustrations. We want everything instantly and as cheaply as possible so there's not enough awareness about where our clothes come from.

How does your role as an art educator contribute to your work as an illustrator, and vice versa?

I have a genuine passion for teaching and being creative is a fantastic way to connect. To know my subject well it's important for me to stay in the loop because illustration develops and changes so fast, and being engaged in my own work makes me feel excited and passionate about my subject, which in turn affects my pupil's enthusiasm. And the kids are always interested in my work, so talking to them helps me come up with new ideas. The two go hand in hand; I can't imagine not illustrating or not teaching.

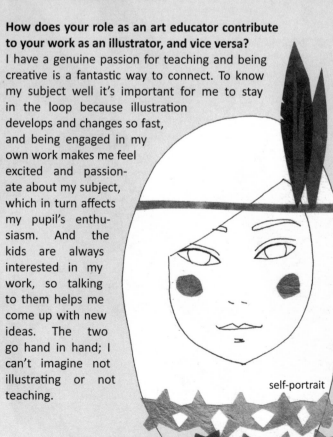

self-portrait

Hannah Marshall S/S 2011

Vintage at Goodwood 2010

Satoshi Date

How do you start to design each new collection?

I usually list ideas that I am wondering about - thoughts about philosophy, science and how we should live - in my note book. Then I pick out the most interesting of these topics. Maybe some philosopher or artist has already found an answer but I like to discover things through my own ideas and research.

In what way does fashion allow you to combine all your creative ideas?

I create artwork in two dimensions as well as making music and video. Fashion feels more real because it is created in three dimensions, and I try to make clothes that combine all the dreaminess and fantasy of my other creative endeavours. I work on music at the same time as I work on designs for my clothing so that it will match the catwalk show when I put them together.

Why did you decide to name your collective after yourself?

We work as a team on ideas that mostly come from my brain. I feel as though I am a percolator, I'm inspired by all the feelings that come from my friends which I filter through my own internal world. Satoshi Date is just a device: percolate Satoshi Date machine and breathe out. I believe that I am connected to everyone in the world and I am just a representative.

How do you work with others to complete each collection?

We get the main idea together and do lots of research before we even think about the clothing. We read, write, listen, draw, collage... developing the idea deeper and deeper. Then we start designing and sampling with textiles and prototypes until the final garments are ready to be made.

How do you balance all the aspects of your creative life?

If I get stuck when I am making music I move onto painting, then on to garment design. Everything relates and harmonises with everything else. I usually find the solution when I go back to the point where I was stuck.

What kind of natural dyes do you use?

At the moment we are experimenting with plants, flowers, onion skins, tea and spices. We are always looking for new methods. We hope to be able to create a collection using only natural dyes.

Where do you source the materials which you upcycle?

Top secret! I use abandoned objects; things I find along the way; items I don't need anymore; broken things. I see potential in what others have discarded.

Why has the UK has been slow to pick up on your work?

I respect working women, but I also admire women who are mothers and homemakers. Sometimes independence can be portrayed through masculinity, and women in the UK often go for edgy, sexy clothing whilst my clothes are delicate and feminine. I think women should be equal to men but that shouldn't mean they have to lose their femininity. And I didn't set out to be a huge overnight success because those people are most quickly forgotten.

How do your garments "continue on their mission to inspire people to think more, care more, be more creative and be more accountable" once they are worn?

My clothes are made from my concept by my hands, unlike mass produced fast fashion about which we often know so little. I think the people who wear my clothes can feel the care that has gone into making them. It may sound like a dream but I think my clothes can be magical, just as other arts such as paintings and music can move us. I don't want my clothes to be merely decorative; I want the wearers to be happy and think about new ideas.

How will you achieve your future goal of having your garments mass produced by "fairly treated and fully appreciated workers in decent conditions"?

We will start from a small team and grow slowly bigger under my leadership. It is important to appreciate and educate my staff, because then they are happier, more loyal and do a much better job. In a regular factory one jacket might be made by up to thirty people but we would like staff to learn all the skills that are required to make the whole jacket. It is better for us and it is better for them.

Would you call yourself an anti-capitalist?

I don't think capitalism is perfect, but I don't think socialism is perfect either. I am against exploitation and greed. I'm not against money because it is a necessity in all societies and it affords education, experiences and travel as well as solving many problems. There is nothing wrong with wanting to make money but I do not believe in doing it at the expense of another person. Unfortunately, greed, exploitation and human rights abuses are often the consequences of capitalism. I think that everyone should gain in any transaction and I think this is absolutely possible if people consider how their actions impact the world.

What are you currently working on?

I am experimenting with cutting my Japanese mind in half and sticking it together with half an English cat mind. Just to see how it works.

Satoshi Date S/S 2011

By Stamo A/W 2010

June Chanpoomidole

You have an incredibly colourful approach to illustration - why do you think that is?

I still wonder about my colourful approach myself. I just love to blend bright complimentary colours of paint. It could be because I am passionate about my subjects and I want to translate this into fresh, vivid and intense pieces of art. I aim to evoke an emotional response from the viewer so it has become something of an obsession of mine to create very vibrant images. I want to make people smile.

How are your fashion illustrations created?

I work at my trusted tiny beechwood desk in the corner of my bedroom, sketching with blue/grey pencils then layering brush strokes on top with slow drying acrylic paints. I love to depict the sheen of satin and the folds in fabrics. Dry brushing creates texture and inks provide detailed marks. It took me awhile to feel comfortable using acrylic paints but I'm glad I persevered.

What kind of music do you listen to whilst you are working?

I listen to all kinds of music while working but right now I prefer Buddhist meditation chants. When I am illustrating a band I like to listen to their music. It sounds clichéed but it means that I can get a feel of the colours as sound, creating splashes, strokes and gradient blends that will best represent the character of the music.

How do you imagine everyday events in a different light?

I quite like to imagine sequential narratives from random things that I see, for example; the business woman I see everyday on the northern line, the scary mannequin in the charity shop, or a man sleeping at the bus stop. I record these moments either in my sketchbook or secretly on my camera phone. I also record quirky items of clothing that stand out to me. I am a very subjective person and I tend to think a lot about everything.

Why did you decide to illustrate the designs of Maxjenny?

As soon I saw the Maxjenny collection I knew my illustrations were perfect to showcase her designs. I love the way she uses sustainable material made from plastic bottles to create clothing that is really stylish and wearable. The innovative simplicity of her simple drapes fold to follow natural body movement and it only feels right to use the strokes of my paintbrush and striking use of colour to emphasis the dynamics of Maxjenny's designs.

How do you fit illustration around the demands of other paid work?

With a lot of determination and flexibility; I try my best to fit illustration around part-time jobs. Everything is really erratic but if I need to I will work late into the evening after I come from work. I buy really cheap notebooks that fit into my pocket so that whenever I get an idea I can quickly sketch it out. I find this really convenient when I am on the go.

What kind of promotion do you do?

I do a wide range of things. I always have postcards and business cards on me to give out to anyone who might be interested and I totally recommend this as one of the most cost-effective ways of promotion because you never know who you might meet. I've met publishers, teachers, engineers and games developers on my travels. I always send a follow-up email when I give out my business card. Promotional mail-outs can be quite costly and whenever I make intricate books I end up wanting to keep them for myself so I need to figure out a more cost-effective method of producing them. A good website is vital because an online portfolio makes it so easy to show work as well as being better for the environment.

Makepiece S/S 2010

Hermione de Paula A/W 2010

self-portrait

How does social networking bring the outside world closer?

It's important to have a good presence on Google searches because this leads the audience to you, so I do lots of collaborative projects, get involved with art swaps, giveaway goodies and I constantly comment on other people's work on blogs and via Twitter. I think you need to be determined to make an impact. I am living back in Cheam Village - which is a quaint suburb of London where I grew up - so social networks allow me to easily connect and communicate with my fellow creatives. I engage with everyone I follow and who follows me, chatting about illustration, random trends or giving tips. It feels good to be involved with others online and makes my days a little nicer.

Why is it so important for ethical fashion to be promoted through illustration?

Illustration is a great way to promote the narrative of ethical fashion in an attractive way; it can be used to describe where the materials come from, who designs the garment and who makes it. An audience will naturally remember a story told via an illustration much more clearly than from a photograph. In my opinion.

Basso & Brooke S/S 2011

Emma Griffiths A/W 2010

Elinor Franklin A/W 2010

Ziad Ghanem S/S 2011

Andre J. at LFW

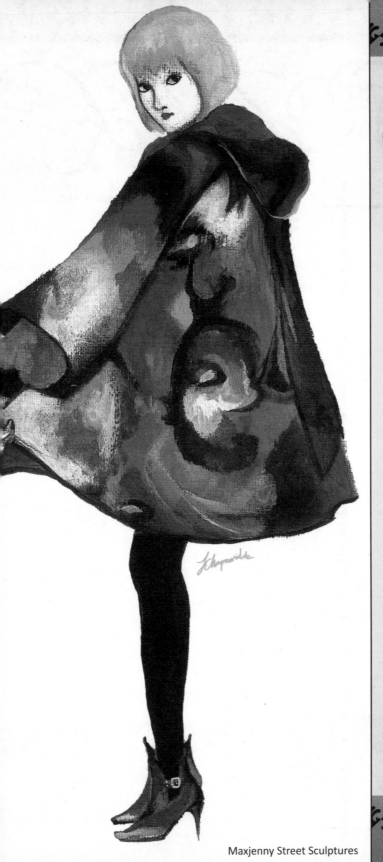

Maxjenny Street Sculptures

Maxjenny

Wearable art.

Maxjenny Forslund was inspired to create her label when she discovered her mother's paintings in the cellar. Her mother Margareta Forslund is also a designer and together they create the bright print designs (some of which are based on self-portraits) that characterise her line of Street Sculptures signature waterproof capes. The capes are based on a circular pattern that drapes over the contours of the body, and are perfect for riding a bike in the rain.

Intelligent sustainable materials.

Maxjenny capes are created from a recycled material made out of plastic PET bottles. Dye sublimation printing is used as an even more environmentally friendly substitute to digital printing. The sourcing of good quality materials is a big part of Maxjenny's job and The New Black diffusion collection utilises 'intelligent fabrics' that react to external stimuli; including bamboo, wool and linen. Leftover fabrics are used in the Maxjenny for Minis kids' collection. This has been a "super duper thing which more people should do."

Moving beyond Denmark.

According to Maxjenny there is little to no support for ethical fashion designers in Denmark, so she has shown at Estethica in London and in Paris. By showcasing where there is a bigger melting pot of creative, open-minded people she hopes to reach a much broader market. Her website also sells organic and fairtrade perfumes, skincare and accessories made by other companies.

Kellie Black

FASHION ILLUSTRATOR

self-portrait

Why do you name yourself Miss Pearl Grey?
First and foremost I like the playfulness of an arty alter ego so I decided while I was at university that my business name would be Pearl Grey Illustration. Pearl is my middle name and Grey is a derivative of my surname. I also have a bit of an Earl Grey tea-drinking habit. The moniker Miss Pearl Grey sprang from all this musing.

Where did you study and what were you taught about the industry?
I took a BA in Illustration at the University of Westminster in London. My work was regularly subjected to criticism, which was good preparation for dealing with clients. I still get together with some of my friends from the course to conduct 'crits' on our work even now we are working professionally. Freelancing can be a very insular affair and I believe it is important to have external, objective opinions from people that I respect. Honing your craft and creating all day every day is a fun but difficult task; it requires a dedication and work ethic far removed from the indulgent carousing that arts students are accused of! There was a great deal of theory on my course and I had to learn how to stay motivated and focused which have been great long term skills. Having said all this, I don't think anything can truly prepare you for working in the industry until you are actually out there on your own.

Why did you decide to become a member of the AOI?
I decided to become a member of the Association of Illustrators when I was a student because they offered discounted entry to the Images competition (and I was then selected for inclusion in the book, which was brilliant publicity at that stage of my career). Since then

I have become a full member. The AOI has provided me with friendly support and guidance as a freelance practitioner, and I am more confident as a working Illustrator knowing that I have the reinforcement of a prestigious and experienced organisation behind me.

Where are you based now and why?

After college I moved back to Sussex to set up my business, but I often travel up to London to meet with clients. I don't ever feel that distant from people because it's possible to be in contact with people all over the world at anytime via the internet. I speak to other illustrators regularly on Twitter and it has been really great for marketing my business: I've gained paid commissions from Twitter.

What is your workspace like?

It is organised chaos! I have piles of paperwork and magazines everywhere, squirrelled away for when I need them. And a huge box full of pencils. I usually listen to jazz while I am working because it doesn't require a lot of attention from me, despite the fact that I often find myself pausing for a moment to enjoy a particular track.

Where do you go for fresh inspiration?

There is no substitute for drawing from real life; if you want to really know a subject you need to observe it. I love capturing the real character of a person through facial expressions, so simply sitting on a bench or in a cafe with a sketchbook never fails to provide illustrative inspiration. And the internet has never let me down yet - I regularly read lots of design blogs and websites and I follow lots of very talented artists on Twitter so I am regularly updated with their new work.

Why do you like doing fashion illustration?

I love everything about fashion, from the very ordinary choices of people on the street to downright ridiculous catwalk extravaganzas. The abundance of colour, patterns and shapes that change from season to season provide a constant source of inspiration for the illustrator in need of a new project.

How does your love of humour translate into your fashion illustration?

I love to make people smile, so I delight in capturing the peculiar and unusual. I think people can take life too seriously, and the fashion industry is no exception; some of the outfits on the catwalks are very beautiful, and some

are hilarious; both of which make great fodder for illustration. Just look at those deadpan looks on some of the model's faces: it's not like anyone would walk down the street in some of the more truly outlandish catwalk outfits.

How does your prop and puppet-making fit alongside your illustration?

Puppet and prop-making are just another means of illustrating. The initial designs are illustrated, and my favourite three dimensional projects are those in which I am involved at every stage, from initial concept to finished product. There is the danger when you do what you love for a living that it becomes just a job, and working in different media means that I stay thankful for the opportunities that arise.

What kind of paid work do you enjoy the most?

It's very liberating when a client asks me to have fun with a project and I am very grateful that I love my work. It's fantastic to wake up in the morning and know that I am being paid to have creative fun. I am currently working on an animation for a comedian and some images for a skincare brand.

How has being part of Amelia's Magazine helped you to develop your work?

Amelia's Magazine champions young creative professionals, so I feel both creatively reinforced and gratified to be featured. It acts as a portal to share my illustrations with people who want to see them and there is no better feeling than knowing I am appreciated. Plus, the tight briefs set by the writers are a great way to explore varied subject matter and learn to manage deadlines efficiently.

How can illustration raise the profile of ethical fashion?

Ethical fashion will struggle to become totally mainstream while it is seen as a separate entity from the rest of the fashion industry. Fashion needs to be ethical as standard but unfortunately most people still have a preconceived idea of ethical fashion as consisting of dull and shapeless hemp affairs without an iota of pizazz. Thankfully some designers are now blazing the trail for ethical practice in high-end fashion, and it is reassuring to see that sustainable fashion is becoming cool and marketable. When something is beautifully drawn it gives the impression that it is covetable, so if ethical fashion can be presented, by illustrators, in the same high esteem as other fashion, then the line between ethical and mainstream fashion will be blurred until eventually there is no longer a distinction.

Nancy Dee S/S 2010

Nancy Dee

Tamsin and Seraphina Davis are sisters in ethical fashion design. Nancy is a long standing family name and Dee simply stands for the initial of their surname, Davis. They settled on the label Nancy Dee because it is a little bit kitsch and reflects the style of their designs.

How did Nancy Dee come about?

Seraphina is my younger sister by four years and she has the background in fashion design whereas I have worked in the film industry and studied economics and social policy, so I am better suited to managing the business side. We started working together because Seraphina wanted to market her designs and she needed a partner. I had just finished my studies and wanted to work on something related to social policy. We launched Nancy Dee in 2008 to create garments that bridge the gap between style, versatility and ethical production.

How do you manage to keep your designs both retro and up to date?

Fashion is cyclical by nature, and all trends are developments on past ideas. We take the shapes and references that appeal to us from history and update them by using new eco fabrics and modern colours. The prints play a large part; they are designed by us but influenced by older designs.

How did you hook up with the family-run factory in India that makes your clothes?

We were actually approached by them whilst at a trade show which was lucky because it wasn't working out with another factory, so we were actually searching for someone to take over production. Fate intervened: we met the owner in London, then travelled over to Delhi later that season to check over the factory conditions, meet the staff and work on samples.

How will you further reduce your environmental impact?

Video conferencing and daily phone calls enable both Seraphina and I to work from home (I live in Leicester while she is in London). Skype is an amazing invention that helps us to keep in touch with the factory, reducing the need to visit so often. We're constantly looking for ways to reduce our environmental impact, such as the use of degradable packaging for the webshop – but it is an ongoing job. We want to start some production in the UK since one of our biggest environmental impacts is caused by the delivery of stock from India. Many UK factories lost a huge portion of their income when it became so much cheaper to produce garments in Asia, so it will be nice to bring some work back here.

What do you predict for the future of sustainable fashion?

There will always be high demand for cheap disposable fashion, which means it will be hard to stamp out worker exploitation completely. We need to fight for sustainability on different fronts; through increased customer awareness, better worker regulation in developing countries (and policing of such laws), and more union power. However, the tide is turning and economic impacts like increasing fuel prices and falling exchange rates are slowly pushing up the cost of production in Asia. I think we will see a revival of the UK clothing industry and new centres of development will emerge in countries like Africa.

How do you work with fashion students and what is the best way for them to approach you?

We have collaborated with students on graphic design projects for prints and website design, and are planning a competition for students to design a Nancy Dee print. We help students with their end-of-year projects, and answer a lot of interview questions for them – the way we see it, they are the next generation of designers so it's important to get them fired up about ethical design. If a student is interested in approaching us, they just need to drop us an email.

Noir

**ETHICAL FASHION DESIGNER:
PETER INGWERSEN**

Peter Ingwersen, creator of the NOIR fashion brand, studied at the Danish School of Design. An internship at Levi's led to twenty years working with the brand, culminating in directorship of Levi's Europe. In 2005 he founded NOIR and the cotton brand ILLUMINATI II, with the aim of combining luxury fashion with ecological responsibility and sustainable practice.

You are known for strong silhouettes and lots of black - what inspires you and who designed the collection?

NOIR is inspired by turning sustainability sexy. My biggest sources of inspiration are Helmut Newton's photographs of strong, sexy women, Victoriana, rock and trip hop music. I work alongside Rikke Wienmann, who I first met at Levi's, and Vibeke Vilken, who started out as a trainee before becoming co-designer on the collections.

Who uses the ILLUMINATI II fair traded and organic cotton fabrics from Africa?

Illuminati II was created to ensure a finer alternative to organic and fairtrade cotton fabrics that were so thick you could smoke them. Today NOIR and our diffusion line BLLACK NOIR use the fabrics alongside a group of B2B corporations which use the cotton in corporate uniforms.

How do you ensure that you stick to your mission, to create a minimum of harm and hopefully to help out the communities and environments in which you operate?

Many suppliers and factories hold certifications today. Otherwise we ask them to sign our code of conduct and then we audit them by visiting them.

What is the most important thing to consider in a sustainable business model?

Rome was not built in a day. It takes time to build a sustainable business model and you need to allow for improvements and constant evaluations to match the latest developments of trade. It's important to focus on where you think you can make a change because it is impossible to alter the entire supply chain in a year.

Have you noticed many changes in sustainable practices?

Cotton growing requires a huge quantity of water which has made me question whether organic practices impact the environment more when compared to the use of manmade fibres. Nevertheless organic farming makes use of compost rather than chemical pesticides, which enhances the percentage of humus in the soil thus making it more able to store a large amount of water. Sustainable practices are constantly evolving.

Piers Atkinson S/S 2011
La Belle Au Bois

J Smith Esquire A/W 2008
Dance With Me

Krister Selin

Krister Selin studied graphic and spatial design at the Senior Secondary School of Art and Music in Savonlinna, Finland. He learnt how to design graphic novels, packaging and typography but realised that his heart was in illustration, so he came to study at the Arts University College at Bournemouth. He firmly believes that having an international degree opens more doors and fortunately he very much likes our language and the sunny seaside culture of his university town.

Krister has been told he is a natural for fashion illustration, so he decided to concentrate on developing his style by working on briefs for Amelia's Magazine. This has given him the opportunity to depict some amazing fashion designs as well as helping to develop his ability to work effectively on briefs that require a quick turnaround.

He works by combining ink and pastel marks with elaborately textured surfaces that are created by folding paper or splashing bleach, always challenging himself to combine unconventional materials and processes. The final image is scanned onto a computer but he does very little digital tweaking because an organic feel is more important to him than a polished one. He feels privileged to interpret fashion designs in his own style, and has recently started to work alongside a fashion designer, incorporating his prints into the collection.

Having grown up with Scandinavian tales of robber girls, trolls and fairies, Krister continues to be inspired by the mythology and folklore of his homeland. The structure and flows of Finnish architecture and product design also remain with him so he was particularly attracted to the By Stamo collection, so full of strong flowing colours.

If possible he will meet a client in person to ensure he leaves a memorable impression. He is extremely hard working and ambitious because he knows how many graduates enter the fashion industry every year, and now that he has a firm network of creative friends he intends to stay in the UK for the foreseeable future.

self-portrait

Charles Anastase S/S 2011

David Longshaw A/W 2010

Where and how were you trained in fashion design?

In Greece I studied hand weaving and embroideries at institutions and museums and with local people so that I could learn about traditional techniques. Then I trained at the London College of Fashion and I have also studied shoes, millinery and textile design for print. Besides having my own brand, I also consult and train on the technical side of fashion; pattern-cutting, garment technology and quality control. I recently set up Ecoluxe with fellow ethical designer Elena Garcia to promote eco-luxury as a lifestyle choice. I am also working on a Masters in Business Administration with the University of Liverpool. I study all the time to keep my mind ticking over.

How do you determine what is ethical in fashion design?

The work ethical comes from the ancient Greek word ethos, which means a combination of honesty, justice and sincerity. According to Aristotle, these moral characteristics were an important aspect of everyday life. My brand practices ethos by using local resources where possible, working with and within the community, developing people skills to create sustainable hand crafted products. For my diffusion line I also source vintage fabrics from redundant stock or end of rolls from warehouses all over Europe - or whichever part of the world I happen to be visiting.

Can you describe how your logo came about and what it means?

My logo is a copy of a crocheted flower that is exhibited in the Cultural Museum of Kefallonia, the Greek island that I come from. The original versions were made from cactus threads and many fine examples were exported to Brussels and France from the 16th century onwards.

How does being Greek affect the way you design?

Designing is more of a way of life and a mindset than a piece of land, but I am fortunate that as a Greek I have a vast history and tradition behind me that inspires and provokes me. I am obsessional, in that I research and collect embroideries and textiles from all over the world and it really helps me to understand the mentality of the people who created and wore them. Greece, or Hellas (as it is has been called for the last 10,000 years) means 'the place of light' and its colours are always full of stories. But then I am madly in love with the British autumn - I collect the fallen leaves in books every year. Call it the best of All Worlds...

By Stamo S/S 2011

Georgina Hardinge S/S 2011

Georgina Hardinge S/S 2011

A.Hallucination S/S 2011

Michael Van Der Ham S/S 2011

Patrick Wolf

Prangsta Costumiers

Fashion designer Martina Spetlova hails from Bohemia in the southern part of the Czech Republic. She studied Chemistry and Biology at university in Prague before coming to London where she was accepted onto a print design BA at Central Saint Martins, despite the absence of a portfolio. Having recently graduated from her MA she is now working on her second collection. En route she has won several prestigious competitions. **Studying for an MA at Central Saint Martins seems to open doors.**

During her year out from Central Saint Martins she set up a fairtrade embroidery network with women in Pakistan, spending six months living in the area to network between communities and fashion designers, which was **great fun but also a lot of responsibility.** There was an exhibition in London but sadly the project didn't last much longer after she left. **I am now busy with my own label but I hope to incorporate similar projects into my work in the future.** Thanks to her print design background Martina is able to fund her label from the sale of her printed textile designs and she also teaches pattern cutting to a small group of ladies.

Her final collection featured interchangeable panels inspired by Lego building blocks, and this idea has become a key feature of her work. **It's a fun and easy way for my customers to create a new look. I like the adaptability and flexibility of linking carefully selected panels of knits, silks and leather using zips.** Zip manufacturer YKK sponsored her MA and S/S 2011 collections. **This relationship is embodied by a jacket I constructed entirely of zips.** She plans to use old stock from YKK for her next collection.

The London College of Fashion's Centre for Sustainable Design has supported Martina to find ways of working sustainably. **I always knew that I wanted to be ethical when I started my own label, but I wasn't sure where to start because there is so much to learn in terms of finding materials and developing production methods.** Her patchwork approach to materials selection lends itself to the use of small quantities of waste and end-of-roll fabrics but to make use of these she needs to start building relationships with the mills. Coming up she also has exciting plans to showcase her work through collaborations with filmmakers and performance artists.

Martina Spetlova

ETHICAL FASHION DESIGNER

Martina Spetlova S/S 2011

Ziad Ghanem A/W 2010

Lisa Stannard

Like me, you specialised in printed textile design at college, where do you find inspiration for your designs?

I take photos of everything; flowers, buildings, interesting people. Whenever I begin a project I look through my pictures and play around with colour and composition. I like Japanese and naive art and I spend a lot of time researching inspirational imagery. I keep up with new developments in textiles technology and current designers such as James Jean whilst also paying homage to the classic designs of Pucci and Issey Miyake. I aim to create traditionally beautiful yet modern textile designs.

How do you create a signature illustration?

I developed my drawing style at university when I was studying printed textile design. We had a lot of drawing classes and I drew all the time. I start by sketching different poses on my graphics tablet, then I choose my favourite and layer translucent colours over the image in Illustrator. My best work always comes when I am able to spend the day alone in my own little world, listening to my favourite music. It can be hard to find this time when I have to run my business but it is a really important part of my practice.

How do you juggle fashion illustration with print and fashion design?

I find that they are mutually complementary and I love doing both; I can design a garment and then draw it as a fashion illustration that is a piece of artwork in its own right, then I can print that onto a t-shirt. It's great when an illustration project gives me an idea for a fabric or dress design and I love creating my own characters.

self-portrait

What are you up to at the moment?
A friend showed me the Supermarket Sarah website, so I sent her some images of my collection and she invited me to join her pop-up shop in Selfridges. Then I was asked to present my own wall. I have also worked as a freelance textile designer, collaborated with American celebrity designer Whitney Port, done a bit of teaching and right now I am interning in the print department for Matthew Williamson. It's great to see how a big studio operates and the experience will not only help me to become a more versatile designer but enable me to set up a successful studio when I return to Manchester. I have done a bit of work with big fashion brands such as ASOS but I am mindful to keep my work quite exclusive.

How does sustainability fit into the way you work?
At the moment it is easy for me to be sustainable because I only make a very limited number of garments but in general I would rather spend more money on good quality ethical production. I want my designs to have longevity, to be kept and cherished regardless of fashion trends. I'd love to collaborate on some print designs with an ethical designer.

Why is it important to work hard and be determined?
A lot of my friends think I'm crazy to work so hard but I don't see it like that. It's important to be committed and make a good impression. I tried to prepare myself when I was at university - I thought that was the hardest I would ever work - but I've been working flat out since I graduated. I find it really rewarding and I will always do my best to complete my work to the best possible standard, whatever the deadline. It's way more satisfying and I am determined to get where I want in the shortest amount of time possible.

You have a very clear vision of what you want - where do you hope to be in ten years time?
I would love to own and run a successful creative business; designing fashion collections, printed textiles and of course making illustrations. In an ideal world I would expand my product base to include interiors, books, and stationery. And I really want to carry on collaborating with other artists, designers and brands.

Zoe Sherwood Graduate Collection 2010

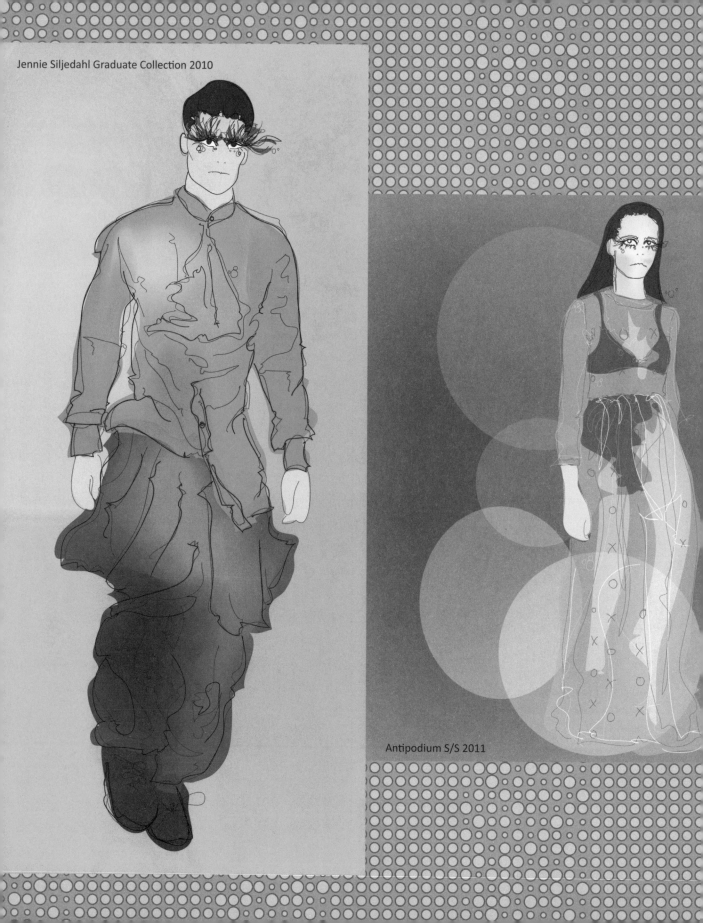

Jennie Siljedahl Graduate Collection 2010

Antipodium S/S 2011

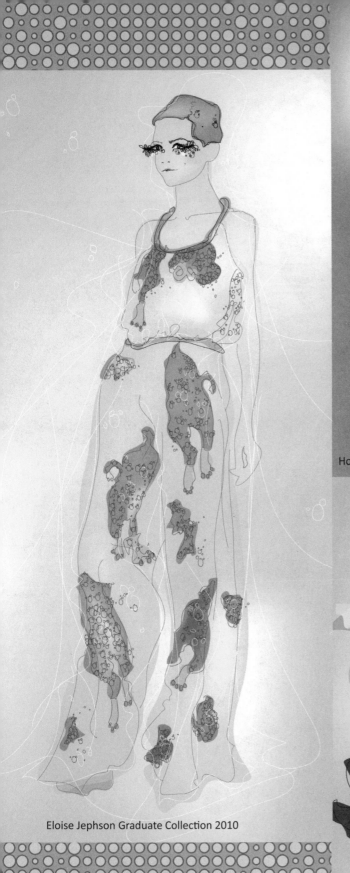

Eloise Jephson Graduate Collection 2010

House of Holland S/S 2011

Emesha S/S 2011

Emesha

Romina Karamanea S/S 2011

Emesha is created by Emese Nagy, who was named after the lead lady in a myth about the creation of the Hungarian kingdom. She grew up between Hungary and the United States before moving to London, all of which has made her very open-minded and observant. **My travels have been a great inspiration to me as a designer.** She particularly likes the quirky style of places such as Shoreditch in east London.

Being a socially sensitive type who wants to help others it was natural that she took an ethical stance for her brand especially as she began to understand more about the origins and manufacturing of clothing. As a strict vegetarian she doesn't use fur or leather in her designs, and only natural materials. An internship at Vivienne Westwood taught her about precision in complicated patterns, and at Jasper Conran she was given the confidence to create a collection from start to finish. **I was involved in all the stages of production which gave me a good insight into how the final garment comes together.**

She makes Sporty-Luxe clothing: featuring clean modern cuts with a touch of menswear styling and a sporty touch. Her S/S 2011 collection was inspired by hanging puppets, primarily Russian artist Alexandra Exter's geometric marionette figures from the 1920's. She works with a pattern cutter and seamstresses in Hungary, and has plans to set up a full production unit that will also be able to provide an ethical service to other labels.

Her recent participation in Eco Fashion Week Vancouver came about as a result of the organisers finding her on the internet. Next up is an exhibition at the Japan Fashion Week in Tokyo followed by a fashion show in Helsinki and she plans to launch a new line soon.

James Hock S/S 2011

Ellen Chatelain Graduate Collection 2010

Lu Flux S/S 2010, Eco Life of Riley

Olivia Rubin S/S 2010

Yelena Bryksenkova

Why is detail so important to you?

For me, the true essence of everything is in the details. It's the truly deliberate things, the result of a choice that, if studied carefully, speaks volumes about the choice-maker. I enjoy drawing detail because it brings life to otherwise mundane shapes; it helps me think of everything as worth looking at. The careful repetition of drawing a pattern is a highly meditative process.

Why did you chose to illustrate Izzy Lane?

I was instantly drawn to Izzy Lane's line of tasteful, cosy knitwear. Complemented by rubber boots, rosy cheeks, and windswept hair, the garments evoke a refreshing stroll through the dreamy Yorkshire landscape, dotted with tidy houses and grazing sheep. The story behind the company is really what moved me: Izzy Lane's mission is to save sheep that "would have been sent to slaughter for being male, missing a pregnancy, being a little lame, being too small, being too old or having imperfections such as a black spot in a white fleece" and give them a happy home. In addition to supporting the ethical treatment of animals, Izzy Lane keeps the British textile industry alive, utilising Victorian machinery, as well as local spinners and dyers. Naturally, the thought of drawing rolling hills of English countryside, fluffy sheep, and knitwear - all for a good cause - sparked my imagination.

What kind of fashion inspires you the most?

I am drawn to fashion that, in a new way, can tastefully echo the styles of the past. I think the best elements from any time period can be brought back as a sophisticated nod to that time, without looking like a costume. I love the simplicity, geometry, and doll-like charm of the 1960's and how perfect it looks now in the hands of Orla Kiely, for example. I think texture is beautiful, especially tweed and thick, knitted wool. I like a clean, tidy silhouette, but sometimes whimsical, over-the-top high fashion - spilling over with frills and patterns - can be just as mouthwatering.

How do you research your fashion illustrations?

Many of my recent fashion illustrations come from interesting and challenging assignments that I completed in my last year at art school. Meticulous research is one of my favourite parts of being an illustrator, so when I have a chance to pick clothes from existing fashion lines to convey the feel of a specific place, time period, or film, I put a

self-portrait

great deal of work into the accuracy of details. It is always a tremendous learning opportunity as well. I like choosing subjects that are aesthetically appealing to me but that I know little about; I feel as though I am exploring the places I am drawing, and in the process I grow to know and love them, which is felt in the final piece.

How have the places you lived impacted your work?

I have lived in Baltimore since I came here to study Illustration at the Maryland Institute College of Art (MICA), from where I hold a BFA as of May 2010. In the spring of 2009, I lived in Prague for five months and studied Illustration at the Academy of Applied and Decorative Arts, which proved to be a turning point in my style. My family is from Saint Petersburg, and although I've never studied there, the city's Silver Age - the World of Art movement of the early 20th century and Diaghilev's Ballets Russes - have had a great impact on my illustrative style. Simply from lifelong exposure to Russian art, small elements creep into my work; someone once pointed out to me that the way I draw noses is very similar to the noses of saints in early Russian iconography. There are several cities in the world that are very important to me, and they have all contributed in big ways to what is now my aesthetic. Prague inspired a more sophisticated colour palette; Saint Petersburg - a kind of inexplicable melancholy and nostalgia, the beauty of things lost, ghosts, memories.

What has inspired you most from your recent travels?

I have long harboured this romantic concept of The North, and the dream finally materialised in a recent visit to Finland, Sweden, and Norway. These places are inspiring to me on many levels. The nature is breathtakingly, painfully beautiful: there is some kind of ancient wisdom in mountains and forests... and looking at them, really looking at them, so that I forget myself, is a very moving experience for me. The other wonder of these northern countries is that the people who live there really see all of this beauty too, and know how to learn from it, and extract from it the simplest shapes and concepts to be applied to everyday life. Scandinavian sensibility and design inspires in me a desire to find a balance in my life and work between my love for objects and a freedom from them.

Where does your very distinctive colour palette come from?
Prior to my time in Prague, everything I drew somehow ended up being very heavy on blue and green, so my illustrations lacked a warmth that I longed for but for some reason could never achieve. Then I went to the Czech Republic, where I saw my first canola field. In my free time I would travel to the outskirts of Prague and sit, for hours, in the middle of a vast sea of yellow, dotted with the reddish orange roofs of little houses. I cannot say that I made a conscious decision just then regarding my colour palette, but something happened; I became more bold with my use of colour, and that warmth that I sought naturally found its way into my work. I now have a very high opinion of the colour yellow. I mix colours intuitively, and I can sense a growing sophistication in my choices that was not there before.

Can you paint a scene of your workspace?
I work at a rather small, red desk. My work is very small and detailed, so when I am in deep concentration, I keep my face close to the tiny task at hand. I use an ancient box of Leningrad watercolour cakes and very small brushes. There is a folded paper towel, a glass jar of water, and a cup of black tea, sometimes with milk, a habit I picked up in London a long time ago, and which always makes me recall cold English mornings. I'm a night owl and can work until dawn if I sense something exciting happening, with my computer in front of me for reference material, or playing music, a favourite television show or film. I usually play films that I can recite by heart, so I mostly just listen to them while I work, even if they are subtitled.

How have your appearances in Amelia's Magazine impacted your development?
I saw my work in print for the first time when I contributed to the Everything is Connected theme in the final issue of Amelia's Magazine, and my recent work for the magazine online has provided excellent practice in responding to art direction and a quick turnaround, without the pressure of dealing with invoices! For a perfectionist like me, having to work more quickly than usual can be scary but ultimately very liberating, as it forces me to find a shorthand for elements that I would normally spend a long time on, drawing out the painstaking detail.

Has anything exciting happened as a result of your social networking?
I only recently became a bonafide Twitter user, and I almost immediately chanced upon an opportunity to have my sketchbooks featured on Julia Rothman's Book By Its

Day Birger et Mikkelsen

Minna S/S 2010

Little Shilpa A/W 2010

Cover. I have also submitted my work to other prominent online places such as Design*Sponge, which really helped me gain exposure among people in the illustration industry and generate a lot of interest in my work. It alerted me to the fact that these opportunities are everywhere, just waiting to be seized. I have always been rather humble about my work, conscious of making sure that it is good enough to make its 'debut', so coming out of my shell has been an eye-opening experience, and I have already landed a couple of major clients along the way. I have not been one to dive head-first into the online world - I've been quite the sceptic - but I am seeing more and more that I can engage with it without losing my sense of the romantic.

What do you love most about being alive in this world?
What I love most about our world is that it has an absolutely endless supply of things to love and be inspired by. It is mysterious, and sad, and beautiful. I love the idea that people with very obscure and specific interests can find others to share them with. Sometimes I hear from complete strangers what they felt when looking at an illustration of mine, and it matches so poignantly what I felt when drawing it; the idea that I was able to establish some emotional connection with a person far, far away gives me an incredible sense of fulfillment. This is how I hope to make the world a better place: in a very tiny way, drawing tiny connections between people, beyond the limits of language or lifestyle...

Eloise Jephson
Graduate Collection 2010

Animal Bandido A/W 2010

Orla Kiely S/S 2011

ETHICAL FASHION DESIGNER:
ISOBEL DAVIES

What was the path to setting up Izzy Lane?

I started an organic food company when I became aware of the hundreds of permitted toxic chemicals used in food production that are wreaking devastation on our wildlife and natural world. Through my work with organic farmers I then discovered what was happening in the wool industry - that farmers were burying and burning their wool because they were paid such a pittance. Because we do not use wool as much as we used to the British textile industry, once the powerhouse of the nation, is on its knees - as are the communities it once supported. I had no training in fashion but I'd always had an interest in clothes which was nurtured when I lived in London as a singer and songwriter and playing in bands as a bass and saxophone player. If you are creative, you tend to be able to transfer that creativity across different media, and I became determined to start a label using British wool.

Your sheep are rescued from abattoirs - it all sounds very romantic, but how do you find them and rescue them?

I physically don't go to abattoirs. I think if I ever saw inside one I would never get over it for the rest of my life. I intervene before it gets that far. I am contacted by breeders who tell me what animals they are sending to slaughter and then I buy them at the market price. I can't refuse any animals once I am aware of them - I feel it is my responsibility to rescue them. Thankfully the rate at which I am contacted has slowed. The shepherd who looks after them rolls his eyes when I tell him a new batch is arriving. He also gets annoyed that I am being made to pay the full price - some of the sheep arrive with health problems which need a lot of veterinary care.

Where are you based now?

I moved up to Richmond, Yorkshire a few years ago and it took some adjusting to - I miss my favourite restaurants, the markets and the cosmopolitan buzz of London. However, I am living in the most stunningly beautiful landscape where I can drive for hours without seeing another car. I love walking in the hills with my black labrador, putting life into perspective, but I still go back to London to go shopping and see my friends. It would have been a different story ten years ago but thanks to technology I can do all my work from here.

How does the landscape and people affect the way that you design?

I think that what one designs comes from many influences, both past and present - most that we are probably unaware of. For example, details of treasured garments from childhood, mother's coat, old black and white films from the 50's and 60's. I am sure the colour palette of the moors feeds into my designs.

How did dairy farmer turned shepherd Ernest Ayre come to look after your sheep?

My first four sheep lived in a paddock at the end of the road but one day they vanished. Ernest, who had adjacent fields, appeared and offered to help find them. He followed their tracks and we found they had gone on an adventure in the woods. I think they'd got lost and found it a bit creepy in the forest at night so they happily followed us back. That is when Ernest fell for the Wensleydales and he offered to take them on... and the next 600.

What has been the most interesting or exciting fact that you have learnt about sheep, since you started working with them so closely?

I find it really fascinating to observe how sheep are really no different to us. They hang around in gangs and sometimes they will single out one particular sheep to chase around the field - but it isn't malicious, they just like larking around. I'm always moved by the bond between a lamb and its mother and siblings. They display real affection towards each other.

Did you ever use Arctic dog hair in your collection?

We have been accumulating the dog hair - which comes to us by boat from Greenland - for some time. We now have a reasonable volume so we will start processing this new 'ethical fur' soon. I'm open to suggestions on any other animal-friendly hairs, for instance there is a manor not far from here that keeps a herd of bison and their hair is beautiful, just like cashmere. Because they keep the bison for meat I'm not too keen on using it... but having said that they are shot dead outright in the field which has to be preferable to the fear and terror of the abattoir, so in some ways bison hair may be preferable to most wool.

Do the farmers who keep sheep think it's odd that you want to rescue them from the abattoir?

I think farmers are more broad-minded than they were perhaps twenty years ago. Farming has had a bumpy ride, what with Foot and Mouth, BSE and price pressure from

Izzy Lane A/W 2008

the big supermarkets. Many are diversifying and looking for other ways to manage their land and buildings in order to derive an income from them. Farmers tend to like their animals and often have great affection for them, so despite being able to send them to slaughter they probably understand what I am doing.

What's the best reason for becoming a vegetarian?

The best reason for becoming vegetarian is to stop the killing of 50 billion farm animals each year. Most of them are subjected to degrading lives of misery, followed by a terrifying death. It is now proven that we do not need to eat meat and a vegetarian diet is much healthier. All animals are our fellow creatures and we have a duty of care towards them. As Ghandi said, a nation should be judged on the way it treats its animals.

Can you tell us a bit about the North Circular project?

The North Circular is going fantastically well. The designs are done by Katherine Poulton and Alice Ashby so my role is more to do with supply of wool, yarn blends and processing. We have just won the RSPCA Good Business Award and have cool stockists around the world such as Colette in Paris, Harvey Nichols, Dover Street Market and Net-A-Porter, so The North Circular is going from strength to strength. We all have input on the direction of the company and Lily Cole likes to get very involved in this too.

The North Circular motto is Knitted by Grannies, Supported by Super-models. Who are the most memorable knitters on your books?

Our fastest knitter lives in the village of Askrigg in the Yorkshire Dales

and she knits so fast that her fingers and the thread are just a blur. She knits whilst watching the soaps, never looking down, and she can make a sweater in under three days. Our oldest knitter is about 94 years old. Going back a few hundred years all the men in the Dales would have knitted as well, as would the children. They would knit on the move and even in bed when it was dark. It was their main income.

Why is it so important to support the British wool industry?

Wool is our locally produced fibre and we definitely need to bring more back into our wardrobes. Buying a British wool garment supports the mills which scour, spin, dye, weave and manufacture, keeping people in jobs and reducing clothes miles. It keeps us warm enough to turn down the heating, thereby helping to drive down energy consumption. Wool has qualities which can't be synthesised - it protects us from the cold, wind and rain and it self-cleans. A wool garment can last for a hundred years and when it is no longer any use it will biodegrade quickly back into the earth.

Why are Wensleydale and Shetland sheep so wonderful?

The Wensleydales are huge, majestic sheep which fell out of favour because modern ovens cannot manage their 'joints'. Now there are only 1800 breeding ewes in the entire world. They have curly, silky locks which fall down to their ankles, producing the best knitting wool in the world. Their wool contains no kemp, the itchy fibre found in most wools, so it can be worn against the skin. The Shetlands are a small primitive sheep that were introduced to the Shetland Isles by the Vikings and they come in a multitude of natural colours which means that their soft, fine fleece can be spun and woven into cloth without the need for dyeing. They are gregarious and cheeky, always escaping from their fields to explore and they are fascinated by all human activity. The Wensleydales love to graze and thrive on lush pasture, but the Shetlands like to eat garden flowers, nettles, gorse, hawthorn - anything but grass - so they live very harmoniously together.

What makes Scottish cashmere goats so special?

Cashmere yarn is one of the world's most luxurious fibres, combed from the underbelly of goats. We have no idea about the animal welfare of cashmere goats in Asia, but small well kept herds of Scottish cashmere goats now exist in Britain. As well as being kept to very high welfare standards they also tend to the land, keeping weeds under control.

Where will Izzy Lane be in ten year's time?

Blimey, I can't even tell where we'll be in six months. Hopefully we will be an internationally recognised brand. I will have bought Scotland and rescued 100,000 sheep to live out their lives there. I certainly hope you won't find me destitute, out with my flock of 5000 grazing the central reservation of the A1. Knowing me, it is likely to be one or the other. But who knows...

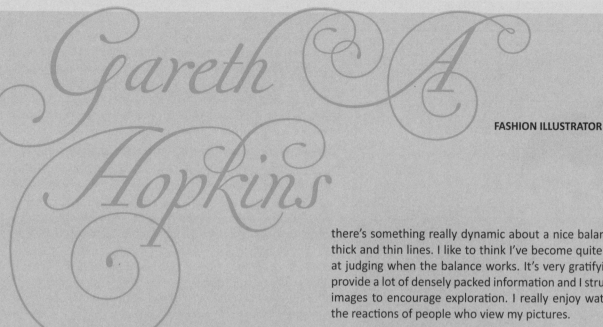

Gareth A Hopkins

FASHION ILLUSTRATOR

there's something really dynamic about a nice balance of thick and thin lines. I like to think I've become quite good at judging when the balance works. It's very gratifying to provide a lot of densely packed information and I structure images to encourage exploration. I really enjoy watching the reactions of people who view my pictures.

What inspires you to create comics?

I've been passionate about comics since I was about twelve years old, but I have no interest in creating comics in the traditional sense so I've been subverting the medium as much as I can. The Intercorstal is an ongoing attempt to create a narrative solely through pattern, contrast and rhythmic layout. It's a project that gives me plenty of scope to revel in over-intellectualising... and I get to play around with my own self-imposed rules – having a comic page made solely of two solid black panels amuses me, if nobody else.

You've only recently discovered fashion illustration - why do you like it?

I see fashion illustration as a collaboration between the illustrator and the fashion designer, and my job is to create an image that shows off the best facets of both our work. Usually my process is quite concept-based, and I get stuck on a set of self-imposed, almost scientific rules to build up a picture. Having to make clothing look good is really liberating, allowing a lot of scope for creativity and experimentation with colour. I love the fact that a fashion illustration just needs to look nice, and I now have a much more finely tuned appreciation for fashion as a whole.

How can we make ethical fashion more commonplace?

A lot of people hear the words 'ethical fashion' and instantly think of unstylish clothes, but this is clearly not true so we need to persuade the general public to get past this idea. Because illustration can be utilised to affect perceptions and alter judgements I think there's a real opportunity for ethical designers and illustrators to work in symbiosis to raise awareness about ethical fashion. It's a perfect way for illustrators to produce satisfying work and raise their profiles: done well it would be a win-win for both parties involved.

Why do you find black lines so seductive?

I'm not sure why black lines have followed me everywhere but they probably allude to my love of comics. I don't really want to dwell on any possible deep-rooted psychological reasons for why I like to block things off... but

self-portrait

Cooperative Designs
A/W 2010

Christian Blanken S/S 2011

Why the A in the middle of your name? In fact, what does Grthink mean?

I include the 'A' in my name because I Googled 'Gareth Hopkins' and found cricket players, physicists, DJ's, acrobats... you name it. To set myself apart I include my middle initial - in my head it gives me a certain Victorian gravitas, but I'm sure others think it's an annoying affectation. Grthink is pronounced 'ger-think' and I invented it as a username on deviantART. As my style has become more defined over the years the word has taken on a life of its own, becoming both a noun, "I'm making a grthink" and a verb, "Sorry, I'm grthinking here". It's pretty ridiculous.

How is life in Essex with your wife and young son treating you?

Essex is mostly great – it's a funny county because it's got a reputation for a particular type of culture, but there's so much more to it than white stilettos and vajazzling. As for balancing my family with work and illustration... I'll be honest, it's not always easy. On a regular weekday I'm away from the house all day at work, then I put my son Bill to bed, sort out the kitchen and only focus on illustration late at night. I usually get to bed really late so I catch up with sleep on the tube. The other main issue to work around is lack of space – most of my tools live in the cupboard under the stairs. I'm not moaning, though – I love everything about my life, especially my family, and even my day job – it's just the way it is. My main tip for anyone else dealing with a similar situation is to make sure your family life is a happy one, because that's going to affect how you feel about everything else.

You're very open on your blog, why do you explain your work processes on line?

I think a good image should speak for itself, but sometimes there's an interesting story behind an image – in the same way that people enjoy behind-the-scenes footage on DVDs, some people might appreciate this for an illustration. My occasional process blogs also act as a way for me to gather up any lessons I've learned along the way. I always write honestly because I think it's more revealing to write 'The outline turned out extra thick because I was laughing at Police Academy' than 'I made this line extra thick' - and yes, that's a real-life example.

How has having an online presence opened up the world?

I entered my first forum when I was fourteen years old, started an online cult during my A-levels and joined deviantART for constructive feedback about my art in a safe environment. By the time I moved over to Twitter I felt much more confident about showcasing my work. A lot of people don't 'get' Twitter because it needs a bit of time investment to get warmed up, but if it's used properly it's an amazing tool for creating a voice, making connections and finding opportunities. I used to chase down projects to take part in but now they come to me thick and fast. I've taken part in shows in London, San Francisco and Glasgow, gained commissions and sold work. I can't bring myself to say no to any offers! At the moment I am preparing for a comics-based gallery show in Holland, storyboarding a film and collaborating on a film. And that's without mentioning all the assignments I pick up for Amelia's Magazine. Being online has given me access to a community of artists that I would never have met in 'real life' and this environment has made me the artist I am today. I can honestly say that if I hadn't taken my drawings online and made such a concerted effort to build up my online presence I would not be making art at all now, and even if I was, I don't think anyone would have taken any notice.

Ross Paul Keenan Graduate Collection 2010

Simone Rocha and Felicity Brown A/W 2010

123

123 Bethnal Green Road recently opened shop after a lengthy renovation of its Victorian corner store in a prime position right at the top of Brick Lane in east London. Hosting three floors of own label designs as well as those of cult designer Noki, what exactly is this new fashion brand all about?

"Some people might think it foolhardy to open an eco-fashion concept store in the midst of the dreaded credit crunch, but so far the reception has been great," says Ross Barry, co-owner with sister Michelle Goggi. Having abandoned their previous careers, in the city and in design and photography respectively, Ross and Michelle are now set to shake up the world of ethical fashion with their 'sustainable canvas' concept. "Ethical, sustainable, green and eco are all terms with very specific connotations. We wanted to do something new and exciting."

With their 123 collection they have created a fresh look, starting with a sustainable (rather than blank) canvas. "Our aim is to make well-made, desirable, British clothing," says Michelle. "We want to extinguish the belief that reusing and recycling materials is at the bottom of the fashion food chain." This is a luxury store selling well designed products that just happen to be ethical as well; upcycled from waste garments and produced locally. Using vertical production methods, whereby an item of clothing can be taken from the cutting table to the store within a week, they are able to provide exactly what the customer is keen on; reacting and responding to new trends within a couple of weeks. Vertical production gives them incredible control over every element of the process and ensures a minute carbon footprint.

LMB Textile Recycling was set up by Ross and Michelle's father Lawrence, who also designed the ubiquitous green textile recycling banks that populate the streets of major cities. As youngsters Ross and Michelle were soon involved in the family business. "Other children got taken to the park at the weekend. We got taken to the sorting factory where we amused ourselves by jumping around in mountains of second hand clothing." Their father's motto was "where possible don't pay someone else to do something you could do yourself" and this belief has clearly been taken to its natural conclusion with the creation of 123 Bethnal Green Road.

Michelle and Ross ensure that the best quality clothing still goes to where it is needed in the developing world, bearing in mind that countries with warmer climates don't want heavier fabrics and are not interested in vintage style prints. Many 123 designs are based around garments which are damaged or not suitable for re-use - for instance they might disassemble a torn leather jacket and remake it into another garment through the clever use of panels. "Obviously there is also the added bonus that the leather is nice and soft where it has been previously worn."

Their in-house design team can be found at their textile recycling factory in Canning Town, east London. "Unfortunately we don't have any glamorous Willy Wonka style sorting contraptions, but our dedicated team of 'pickers' grab out all the most lovely pieces for our vintage department." They also put aside the most gorgeous fabrics, cataloguing them by material and style for the design team. Because supplies are limited all 123 garments are made in small runs. "Sometimes we design with the material we have in mind and sometimes we throw caution to the wind and hope we'll find material to fit a particular design."

123 Bethnal Green Road was once, infamously, occupied by an illegal gun dealer. "We went to look at the property and instantly fell in love with it even though it had been left to rot," says Michelle. "As Lawrence said to us, there's only ever going to be one corner of Brick Lane and Bethnal Green Road." Now the whole parade of shops is getting a facelift in advance of the Olympic Games. Behind the main frontage is a building affectionately termed the Scout Hut. Unfortunately there is little evidence to suggest that it was ever a scout hut, bar a small rotten flag pole on the outside. "That's good enough for us; urban legend seldom requires much more." Rumour has it that the infamous Kray twins were cub scouts here. Times have certainly changed; a few legendary Vintage for Sale pick'n'mix events were held in the Scout Hut before it was refurbished, and now there are plans to host a whole array of events; from the launch of this very book to pop up shops, film nights and exhibitions.

Noki is a long term collaborator: LMB supplies the fabric and he works his inimitable magic. A recent press release states that 123 Bethnal Green Road intends to make sustainable fashion fierce. "Most people's idea of ethical fashion involves an eco warrior in tie-dyed hemp clothing; in order for it to have any longevity it must be accepted on its own design merits." And in the pipeline? New stockists for 123 beyond their flagship store, a new sustainable jewellery range, tentative steps towards homeware and furniture, not to mention further exciting designer collaborations, including one with knitwear supremo Craig Lawrence.

Noki

Noki, aka JJ Hudson, attended Edinburgh College of Art in the early 90's. **I was TOLD I had to take a year out because I had institutionalised behavioural problems and I disturbed the tutors. Enough said...** He thinks in retrospect that he should have joined the Fine Art department where Keith Farquhar and friends were busy pioneering installation art, but being set back a year prepared him well to fit into London's Shoreditch renegade art community circa 1995.

His final degree collection made use of discarded silk screens from the textile department to create a massive sculptural dress and full bustle skirts. Already he was looking for ways to reuse fabric, taking a flawed blue cotton bale and utilising the white streak that ran through it as the basis for a bleached flame-like textile design. Even the waistbands were made by sewing together vintage underwear ribbons to create a simple draw string. **Noki thinking has always been there, even if it didn't have a name.** He likes to work with the rejected elements of a brand, recreating the fabric to make a new statement, working with pre-landfill dead stock to make "über limited edition silhouettes". Dr.Noki's NHS House of Sustainability was originally created for Lulu Kennedy's Fashion East platform and Noki describes it as "a challenging one-off street couture collection" for everyone who realises that fashion is not fair. **The Noki customer is NOT on a Race to Consume.**

LMB Textile Recycling was the place he always hoped to find. **It's an amazing family run company in east London. You couldn't get more British roots with which to establish the NHS Fashion House.** LMB kindly took Noki under their wing, allowing him a free rein to create his NHS vision as the concept for 123 Bethnal Green Road began to develop. **I take my New Era cap off to them for the industrial commitment they have put in.** He is very proud that industry and art have found a way to work creatively together. The opening of the independently owned 123 Bethnal Green Road store is hopefully a signal that the times are a-changing.

Noki is an artist and an activist who gives a fuck about caring, and as a result he has a very large, dedicated and recognisable fan base. **I create one-off Noki 'hamburger-bricks' to throw around wildly. I hope they make a smashing impact.** He is particularly pleased with the creation of the care label that appears inside all NHS garments, 'Created with Dr Noki's Sustainable Canvas'. **Having this officially sewn into every garment creates a strong Noki-Art Value for every patient.** And if any later alterations are needed there is always Dr Noki's Aftercare Service, whereby he will personally re-customise any clothing. Though he does warn that the aftercare "can be a pretty extreme diagnosis".

Noki A/W 2010

Hat by Barbara Keal

Morphe A/W 2010

Charlie Boots
S/S 2010

self-portrait

Naomi Law

How do you create your illustrations?
I work with a combination of watercolours, ink, aquarelle pencils and masking fluid to make basic shapes, textures and details. I then scan these and work on about fifty layers in Photoshop with a Wacom tablet. All my illustrations are currently done at my dining table in my flat in Hackney, usually working late into the night when I get home from my day job. I hope to graduate to a better surface in the near future: my Dad is building me a special wall-mounted folding desk that I dreamt about.

How did you get into illustration?
My degree was focused on corporate graphics and after three years of designing logos I was fed up with being told exactly what to do and how to do it. I wanted to let my ideas run in their own direction but when I started to take a more illustrative route my tutors were not impressed. I started working in fashion when I moved to London a few months after graduating, initially in sales, then in-house graphic design. I fed my creative appetite by running a small jewellery business in my spare time, making accessories and laser-cut acrylic jewellery which I sold on a stall at Sunday UpMarket on Brick Lane. I still did a bit of drawing here and there, but I really got back into illustration when my friend, Amelia's Magazine fashion editor Matt Bramford, suggested that I did an illustration for one of his articles.

How has being online helped?
I've been doing as many illustrations for Amelia's Magazine as I can, as well as submitting work to other open briefs and competitions that I've found online via Twitter and blogs. I spent quite lot of time finding the right people to follow when I first went online, but everybody has been really helpful and it's so easy to do from home; there's no need to go to networking events or spend loads of money on magazines. I've been actively looking for collaborations and recently worked on some wall graphics for a friend who's launching an interior decoration brand.

What inspires you about a fashion design?
I study the shape of the garment, how the fabric hangs on the body and where I can show draping and movement, looking for interesting details that I can make into a feature. I love the challenge of creating a visual explanation of a garment... finding different materials and techniques to illustrate the details, fabric, weight and shape of a piece while remaining true to the original design. I really enjoy working on illustrations for London Fashion Week for Amelia's Magazine, especially going to the shows in person, which is a very different experience to looking at photos because it gives an idea of how the pieces move. The challenge of quick deadlines makes me much more productive otherwise I'm quite good at procrastinating.

How can illustration help to promote ethical fashion design?
Looking at an illustration gives the viewer the opportunity to see a design through someone else's eyes, which could show them something they might not necessarily have noticed in a photograph. It's a bit like listening to someone's description of what they found most intriguing about an outfit, rather than reading a basic rundown of fabric, colour palette and silhouette.

Hannah Marshall A/W 2010

Joanna Cave

Jewellery designer Joanna Cave makes delicate pieces for the self confident and elegant woman. She met PARTIMI designer Eleanor Dorrien-Smith at London Fashion Week and the pair clicked instantly. For S/S 2011 they have collaborated on a special collection.

Has your Greek upbringing influenced your designs?

I believe that our surroundings influence us a great deal and my Greek upbringing has definitely played its part. My latest collection was purely influenced by the surroundings where I designed it on the Greek island of Tinos, so amongst my inspiration was the beautiful Cycladic landscape and deep starry nights.

Why you currently based in Athens?

I studied in London but after many years I felt I needed a change, and Athens seemed like a pretty exotic destination after a cold and cloudy summer in the UK. It can be difficult since I'm part English and absolutely love London, but Athens has a great tradition in jewellery and it is full of charming little workshops that have been operating for generations. It all kind of fell into place.

Have you always been ethical in your approach to design or did you have an epiphany, and if so what prompted that?

I've almost always used recycled silver. One year I used coral for my collection which is terribly bad - as soon as I found out how endangered coral is and how much damage is caused by extracting it, I completely banned it from my production. That prompted me to find out more about where my materials come from, and I started to look for ethically sourced pearls.

How are Japanese Akoya pearls ethically produced?

The pearls are grown according to local environmental capacities, so the number of oysters per hectare of water is decided according to the natural biodiversity of the area where they are farmed. The pearls are not subjected to the high level of chemical bleaching and colouring that other pearls experience, and the workers are looked after and salaried according to international standards.

Some of your recycled silver comes from the old stock that your father kept in his shop. Where does the rest of your silver come from?

I buy recycled silver from a place that melts old unwanted

Bora Aksu S/S 2011

Joanna Cave S/S 2011

jewellery and other objects to resell. They don't always have enough in stock so sometimes I have to wait for it.

Will there be more collaborations in the future? If so who would you like to work with?

I hope I will continue to collaborate with PARTIMI because we make a great team and our styles really complement each other. I also love Stella McCartney and would love to make a line of jewellery for one of her collections.

How would you define perfect simplicity?

A perfectly round silver disc that's been brushed and given a matt finish. And a wooden floor that's been painted white.

Romina Karamanea

ETHICAL FASHION DESIGNER

Romina Karamanea S/S 2011

You often mix the fluid and the sculptural in your designs. What are the influences behind this?

I design for a woman of balanced contradictions: she is tough and she knows what she wants, but at the same time has a soft introspective side. Also imprinted in my memory are the poetic landscapes of Greece: the severe rocks against the soft sky and the crystal waters. I feel privileged to have been born and raised in such a beautiful country as Greece, and the inspiring landscape has contributed strongly to my aesthetic. I like to keep colour to a minimum because I aim to balance proportion, shape and shade. Innovation in cutting is a paramount feature of my work.

You had an unusual childhood, can you tell us a bit more about your parents' boutiques?

My father was an established TV and radio producer in Greece back in the 60's and the 70's. He was also a songwriter and worked closely with my mother, who was his manager and PR. Together they organised the most successful pop and rock music festival in Greece and in the late 70's they decided to open their first boutique, followed by the second one shortly after. I realise that they did not have standard jobs but my childhood was most fun and action-packed. From a very early age I was involved in the business during my spare time: assisting with sales, buying and helping to build the very fashion-forward window fronts. My parents appreciated my enthusiasm and in return I got whatever I wanted from the stores - within limits - so I had the most amazing teenage designer wardrobe full of Junior Gaultier, Valentino, D&G, Ralph Lauren, Nike and Adidas trainers, Quicksilver surf gear and Diesel and Levi's jeans to name a few.

How did they encourage you to pursue a career in fashion?

They were an inspiration around me 24/7: passionate, hard working with innovative ideas and a real desire to offer something exciting to their customers. I was lucky to have parents that excelled in both creativity and communications. During this time I won a children's award for fashion illustration storytelling which for them was a confirmation that I was serious about moving into fashion design. They decided to invest in private lessons with established artists so that I could learn all the classical principles of drawing and painting: I knew I was very lucky to be in that position and I really appreciated the gift. At the age of twelve I stated my plan to travel abroad, study fashion design and train with the best. They believed and trusted in me and were supportive of my decision however much they hated the thought of me living so far from home.

What sensational ideas have come from a truly unspectacular moment?

Ideas can come from anywhere, and every time I leave the studio I see something that literally stops me in my tracks: a half-finished building construction, a peeling broken surface or reflections on the canal. The difficult part is filtering them! For A/W 2011 I had a fascination with aerial photography where it is possible to see the intricate patterns in street formations. This season darkness and shadows were a big inspiration, as well as geology. My print ideas solidified when I saw the varied shades of horizontal lines in a section of cut away ground on a construction site near the studio.

Why do you predict a more unisex approach to fashion design?

My clothes fuse elements from both sexes; I think that in general people are bored of overt sexual references and obvious fashion revivals, so we are going to see more ambiguous and androgynous fashion, with styles that blur the line between genders and sexualities. For S/S 2011 we played with the man's classic white shirt because woman love this look. But I do have my girly moments; I just had a pastel pink toner put through my hair.

You have a very high profile for a new designer - what is your advice for other up-and-coming fashion designers?

To be a successful fashion brand it's important to maintain a very fine balance between art and industry: there must be pieces within the collection that the press will love, alongside pieces that are commercially attractive to buyers. This is a challenging process but one that I have identified from the start. When I was small a dear family member said to me that I must always be positive, patient and persistent, and I think this is perfect advice for any aspiring new designer.

How has the Centre for Sustainable Fashion helped you to establish low impact manufacturing?

As an overall vision we adhere to creating timeless styles for desirability and durability, but the centre has also inspired us to try and reduce our carbon footprint. To be sustainable it is important to plan, so we have been visiting fabric fairs to research the qualities of exciting new fibres like bamboo, fish skin, peace silk, milk jersey and organic cotton. In the studio we have a zero waste fabric policy whereby we employ clever lay-plan techniques to utilise all fabric, for example in accessories. We also reduce the number of seams by joining pattern pieces where possible to reduce cloth wastage. For S/S 2011 we also used digital printing, which is more sustainable as it reduces water wastage.

What other sustainable practices do you plan to implement?

There is still a lot to be done. I am trained in Lectra CAD/CAM systems so we would like to invest in this software for our studio to increase accuracy, reduce our use of paper, and ensure better lay planning for production. We are also researching how we can work with computer software to reduce raw material wastage at the factory manufacturing stage.

What is the best tip that you have learnt that you can pass onto other young designers considering how to design in a more sustainable fashion?

As a young company it is possible to implement many small, cost-effective sustainability practices; from the recycling of paper, plastic and cloth, to the use of crease-resistant easycare fabrics to reduce energy from ironing. These can be washed at 30 degrees Celsius and lower, so there is a domino effect in addressing climate change because the customers will also be able to save energy.

For up and coming designers it would be incredibly inspiring to know that an edgy designer like yourself is working towards sustainability in design. Do you plan to talk more about your ethical practices?

We are actually about to add information about our sustainable practices on the official Romina Karamanea website and we are about to introduce a small range of one-off pieces created from the offcuts of our last few collections. The brand was nominated for the Innovation award by the Ethical Fashion Forum and we were selected to showcase our S/S 2011 collection at Estethica with the Centre for Sustainable Fashion. We are very proud to have been selected as an inspiring emerging designer brand, and our goal is to create exciting market opportunities as the business grows in a dynamic and sustainable manner.

Maxjenny A/W 2010

KTZ S/S 2011

Ziad Ghanem A/W 2010

Coco Chanel & Igor Stravinsky

Amy Martino

FASHION ILLUSTRATOR

self-portrait

Amy Martino worked in graphic and web design for six years before deciding to go freelance two years ago. "To be honest, the highlight of my professional career was when I decided to go freelance and take control over my time," she says. "Being my own boss allows me to pursue other interests such as illustration." Now she has an outlet for her creativity whenever she chooses and her illustration has already been featured in magazines, blogs and on t-shirts for pro-snow-boarder clothing company Nikita, which perfectly suits her since she is a snowboarder herself. With fashion illustrations she loves to work with forms and colour, exploring the overlap between the process of fashion design and illustration.

She will often have a colour scheme in mind before she sits down to create an illustration. "I always get stuck on colours wherever I am - I could just be on the subway and see someone's socks and it's just this most incredible colour combination which I can't get out of my head." Two days later she'll use those very same colours, treating her computer as a sort of moving sketch-book on which she draws colourful forms from which she gradually teases the right shapes. Because she is interpreting someone else's ideas she approaches fashion illustration with the concept that it should never be a literal represen-tation, but rather an explosion of what she can pull out of the designer's vision. "If it's expected to see two eyes and a mouth on a face then I reject it. Likewise if clothing is supposed to cover one part of the body I'll put it on another." In Il-lustrator she considers body shape and position before drawing the clothing on top and adding layers and texture in Photoshop. She deliberately picks out garments that enable an exploration of the designer's ideas with abstract decorative elements, and with no context for background the form then becomes the entire piece.

Amy chose to illustrate Andrea Crews because the label is known for interesting catwalk shows and poking a little fun at the fashion industry. "I was inspired by the playful theme of going off piste in the winter HORS PISTES col-lection because that's where you find the good stuff." She likes to create art that is silly, inspired and as weird as possible, and finds that if she gets too serious her artwork becomes less approach-able - so she tries to soak up as much creativity as possible because "if I am a boring uninteresting person, my illustrations will be too."

Central Saint Martins Graduate Collection at Latitude

Andrea Crews

Ziad Ghanem A/W 2010

Maroussia Rebecq arrived in Paris in 2002. Deciding that she did not want to work alone she created a fictional character, Andrea Crews, around which she began to build a network of accomplices. Maroussia may be the founder and director but Andrea Crews is a project in which many others take part. Andrea Crews is an avant-garde movement based on a sustainable aesthetic, communicating creative ideas via ethical means. The latest collection is described as "a galactic warrior on a sunset ride".

The average Andrea Crews customer is "good looking and open minded with good style, aged anything from 7 to 77 years old." The antithesis of sleek French fashion, Andrea Crews revels in the juncture of performance art and fashion, playfully recycling unwanted clothing. The crew sorts through old clothes, hunting out the boldest colours and best quality materials. Styles are combined to create "fresh, sexy, unisex, colourful, graphic, funky" outfits, which take shape as they grow. Andrea Crews collections are always accompanied by a big performance and lots of partying - "we work hard, we party hard" - collaborating with other experimental contemporaries on the cultural scene: artists, stylists, video directors and DJs, not to mention musicians. They have dressed Santigold, Metronomy and Yelle.

One of their most memorable parties was in 2005. For the infamous Nuit Blanche catwalk show Andrea Crews ordered five tonnes of second hand clothing and built a 100m catwalk outside in a very popular district of Paris. The crew took people from the streets and dressed them up, sending them down the catwalk every hour for twelve hours all night. They were inundated with people who wanted to participate.

In 2007 Andrew Crews were invited to do a joint performance with Yayoi Kusama, Dot Obsession, at the WIELS art centre in Brussels. A team of dancers dressed in Andrea Crews reenacted Yayoi's feverish childhood hallucinations, ending up in a naked, writhing moshpit. As part of the event Andrea Crews also hosted a clothing reconstruction workshop for the local children, who designed their own mini collection.

For the last winter collection, HORS PISTES, Andrea Crews enlisted the help of a technical team to create a snow storm inside the Centre Pompidou during Paris Fashion Week. Models braved the snow in front of a digital projection as beatboxers provided the apocalyptic sounds. The show ended with the models collapsing under gold sheeting, followed by a performance of traditional African songs, much to the bemusement of the attendant Parisian fashionistas.

Maroussia would prefer to work only with organic fabrics, but is happy to use synthetics - such as those provided by long term collaborator Nike - in her recycled collections. She has worked on a couple of capsule collections with Nike and has also collaborated with La Redoute to reimagine an end-of-line men's pullover as a mini dress. Despite worries about the commercialisation of her brand Maroussia has big plans to create an explosion of creativity across the world.

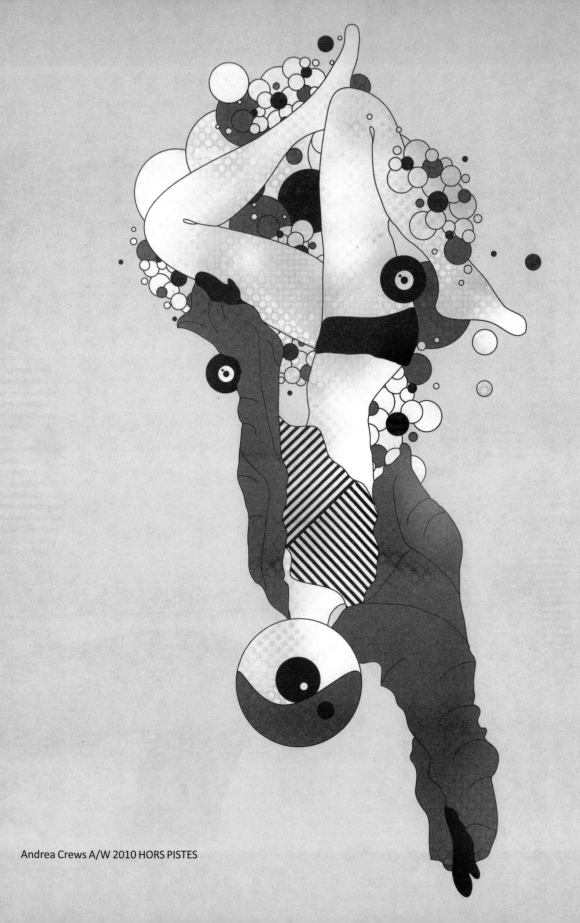

Andrea Crews A/W 2010 HORS PISTES

Andrea Crews A/W 2010 HORS PISTES

Michelle Urvall Nyrén

self-portrait

How does fashion illustration compliment your work as a textile designer?

My watercolour illustrations and my textile work are quite separate to me but both are equally important for my creative inspiration. When I am designing textiles I am a total perfectionist but I am more relaxed with my illustrations, so they give me a bit of space to breathe. To begin with I illustrated mostly for friends, but then someone put some work on Facebook and I got some more commissions from that. I really like the subjects that are covered in Amelia's Magazine so it has been a good creative challenge to contribute my illustrations, as well as a great way to learn how to work professionally and to be seen.

How do you build up an illustration?

Firstly I always pick out an expression in the face or pose to emphasise an impression I get from the garment, then I pick out details from the clothing, using just a few lines to portray the garment in ink or charcoal. I add watercolour quite quickly and scan the image straight into the computer once it is dry.

Why is fashion "culture, communication and storytelling"?

When I'm designing a fashion collection I try to express the personality of a particular character through my choice of colour, material and silhouette, so that when people see my clothes they think twice. Fashion is present everywhere, all of the time, so it is a very important cultural phenomenon through which to make a statement, like music and art.

Why do you prefer working on menswear in your fashion design?

When I started working with menswear it was a huge relief for me because I no longer felt the need to create clothes I would want to wear. Being less limited by my own vanity enables me to create something much more interesting. Again, I am less hard with myself when it comes to illustration, so I find it easier to work with the female figure.

Why did you decide to study in Paris?

I went to Paris directly after high school because I have family there. At that time I was very naive, and easily charmed by the clichéed beauty of luxury fashion. Once I understood more about the industry I changed my idea of how I wanted to work with fashion and decided to study Arts and Craft at Steneby, part of the University of Gothenburg University. It seemed more free and open to me.

Why did you decide to come to London?

I like the simplicity of Swedish design but London is very open minded in comparison so it makes me far more experimental. I am currently on an internship at Mark Fast where I have been learning some very special techniques with unusual fabrics. Afterwards I will present a new textile project that may well be inspired by the things I've learnt at Mark Fast.

Why did you choose to illustrate Dem Collective?

Dem Collective visited my school to give a series of lectures explaining every single step of their production from start to finish. Many designers work with organic materials, but they don't think about the factories or transport. Dem Collective consider every single part of the process, which is really inspiring and impressive because that's really really hard to do, particularly since it isn't a very big company.

What are your views on sustainable design?

It is something that all the schools in Sweden are talking about right now: how we can work with design in a world where we don't really need to produce anything new. At my school in Gothenburg everything is checked for environmental certification, from the food in the canteen to the lights in the buildings. We are encouraged to use recycled materials where possible, and organic materials if we need to work with something new.

How do you consider sustainability in your collection?

I don't have garments in production yet so it is still easy to see exactly where everything is sourced from and I try to re-use and recycle materials where possible. Because the situation is becoming critical, I think it's really necessary to think about the consequences of design.

Holly Fulton S/S 2011

Cooperative Designs S/S 2011

Aminaka Wilmont A/W 2010

Carlotta Actis Barone S/S 2011

Lu Flux A/W 2010, Dame & Knight

Anne Karine Thorbjoernsen
Graduate Collection 2010

Gabby Young

219

Dem Collective

Camilla Jernmark for Dem Collective A/W 2009

**ETHICAL FASHION DESIGNERS:
ANNIKA AXELSSON & KARIN STENMAR**

You were founded in 2004, with the aim of becoming a profitable company that treated people and environment fairly. How have you put this into practice?

We are very close to the whole production chain, from the cotton fields in Gujarat to our ready-to-wear garments. We have also started our own garment factory in Sri Lanka, where we can ensure good salaries and working conditions. All our fabric is fairtrade certified and eco labelled.

What defines a Dem Collective garment?

The design is very important - we make good-looking clothes that customers want. To be frank, the least environmentally friendly garment is the one that no one wants to wear... so our clothing is basic, timeless, and of good quality. We are happy that our customers call us and tell us that a t-shirt they bought five years ago is still in use, and hasn't fallen apart, or gone out of fashion.

Who are the designers you work with? How do the collaborations happen?

It is an important part of the Dem Collective ethos to work with a string of different designers; Maja Jakobsson, Maria Andersson, Camilla Jernmark. Our latest collaboration is with Josefin Lassbo. Both Karin and myself are very open about our lack of design experience, so we like to work with others. Most of our collaborations start out with the designer contacting us.

Why is it a bad idea to use genetically modified cotton?

There is still not enough data on the impact of genetically modified crops on the environment, the soil and the people. But one thing we do know is that they provide three harvests a year and that is really draining on the soil, which means increased use of pesticides and chemicals. And designer seeds are hugely expensive so farmers are more likely to fall into debt.

How do you ensure that no one has been exploited along your supply chain?

We cannot be everywhere, all the time, so we decided to use fairtrade and eco certified cotton only. But at least once a year we visit the cotton fields in Gujarat, meeting with Mr Aryan Bhai, Hema Behn, and the other cotton farmers. We also go to the ginning in Aurungabad, and the spinning, dyeing and knitting units in Tamil Nadu, where our fabrics are made. And of course we are sure that no one is exploited at our own factory in Sri Lanka. But we don't have control over how the lorry drivers are treated or the people working at the freight companies. In the future we will strive to know our whole supply chain, but for now we are proud of having done as much as we have.

You cite corruption as a huge barrier to sustainable practice - how can big companies prevent corruption within their manufacturing flows?

Corruption doesn't just happen, it is always due to human action. It takes place because of greed and prestige. It is really difficult to get rid of corruption but transparency is a good first step in the fight against corruption. Show what you do, and do what you say you do.

DEM means Don't Eat Macaroni, which refers to some graffitti urging people not to eat fast food. How does one fight the culture of fast fashion?

You can't - fast fashion is fast fashion. What we can do is work with the concept of slow fashion, where people and environment come first. This of course means that we cannot always follow the latest colour and design trends, but we can create our own trend, where colours are environmental friendly, fabrics are 100% eco, and good design champions over constant change.

How do we shift the current profit-making paradigm of the corporate world towards something more sustainable?

All companies have to make a profit or they are not economically sustainable - but big corporations need to learn how to see the long term perspective. Profit is not just counted in currencies: environmental disasters and human suffering are for real and no one will make a profit if our world falls to pieces. The current economic paradigm is very much a one-sided power struggle but we work with the concept that everyone should benefit from our business.

What will Dem Collective be working on next?

For now we will continue to dig were we stand. We have laid down a large foundation and now we are working on the house. So far our main markets have been in Sweden and a few of the Nordic countries, but we are now aiming to go further abroad. Our brand is registered in the US, and it will be very interesting to investigate if/how we can find a market over there. We are also expanding our designer branch, with several interesting collaborations in the pipeline. We hope to expand our factory in Sri Lanka; it will make us very happy to employ more well looked after staff.

Cooperative Designs S/S 2011

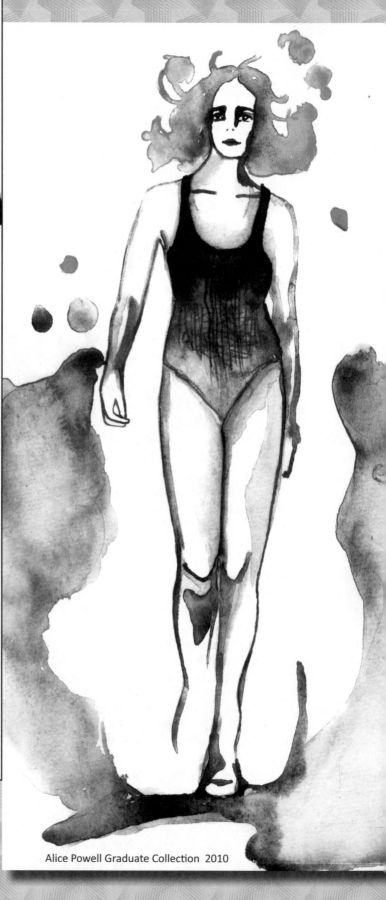

Alice Powell Graduate Collection 2010

Alice Powell Graduate Collection 2010

Dem Collective A/W 2010

Ziad Ghanem S/S 2011

Ziad Ghanem S/S 2011

Michelle Lowe-Holder

ETHICAL ACCESSORIES DESIGNER

Canadian Michelle Lowe-Holder completed an MA in knitwear at Central Saint Martins and launched her eponymous collection in 2001. She has always included sustainable elements in her collections, but having children made her think more deeply about her long-term impact. Being mentored by the Centre for Sustainable Fashion was hugely influential in persuading her to work in a fully ethical manner.

Michelle quickly realised that she had always been most interested in the details, so she decided to concentrate on designing accessories in heritage craft styles from all the offcuts that had accumulated in her studio over the years. She has collaborated with photographer Polly Penrose to showcase her new accessories collections through images of unusual beauty. For her first lookbook the pair explored beauty taboos in fashion - age, youth and the fuller figure. For the second collection they worked with a circus performer to explore body shapes that could be either awkward or beautiful. She plans to keep experimenting with imagery that is not inhibited by the normal boundaries of fashion, and hopes that all types of people will feel empowered by wearing Michelle Lowe-Holder accessories.

Michelle Lowe-Holder S/S 2011

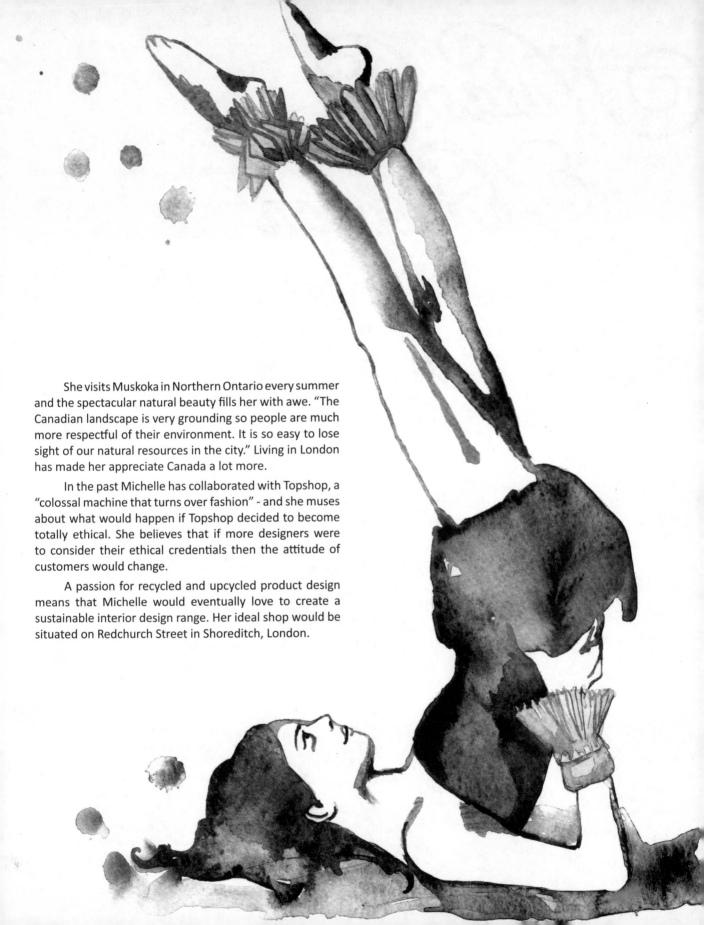

She visits Muskoka in Northern Ontario every summer and the spectacular natural beauty fills her with awe. "The Canadian landscape is very grounding so people are much more respectful of their environment. It is so easy to lose sight of our natural resources in the city." Living in London has made her appreciate Canada a lot more.

In the past Michelle has collaborated with Topshop, a "colossal machine that turns over fashion" - and she muses about what would happen if Topshop decided to become totally ethical. She believes that if more designers were to consider their ethical credentials then the attitude of customers would change.

A passion for recycled and upcycled product design means that Michelle would eventually love to create a sustainable interior design range. Her ideal shop would be situated on Redchurch Street in Shoreditch, London.

Natasha Thompson

FASHION ILLUSTRATOR

self-portrait

Natasha goes under the pseudonym Natasha Likes Tea, as well as the Secret Tea Party. And she's just joined the Tea and Crayons collective of illustrators. There seems to be a bit of a theme here…

I love tea; my friends think I'm obsessed.
I have hundreds of different types of teas, and I really like Alice in Wonderland, hence the name of my website. The best way to ponder over a blog is with a nice cup of tea, usually English Breakfast if it's early in the morning, with my curtains wide open to let in the early light. It's usually quieter at this time so I find it best for reading.

It's important to source materials as ethically as possible if you're an illustrator.
It shows you're bothered about what is happening in the world around you. Collaging with found papers is an essential element of my work. I don't waste anything, and I always reuse leftover papers in any way that I can. Everything is scattered across my desk; pens, stacks of old books and magazines. I am an obsessive collector and I always start an illustration by sifting through my references until I find something out of which I can develop my work.

I like to draw on my own experiences.
I like to leave invisible references in my work; sometimes I will include a particular word that I remember from a past conversation, or a colour that I find in a paper that I've kept for a long time. I like to be playful, and I feel my sense of humour comes out naturally within my illustrations. I don't like anything that is too serious and sombre.

Working quickly is a great way to process ideas.

When I start a fashion illustration I focus on the clothing so that I can exploit the best colours, textures and tones. If I can create something beautiful then people will be more likely to engage with it. Working with Amelia's Magazine has been brilliant for my portfolio because good quality is expected and that's what I will churn out. Learning to work with a quick turnaround means I have to get on with it - which is important practice because at the end of the day that's what people will pay me for.

Tea and Crayons on Twitter.

My collaborative illustration venture has been put together with five other lovely Twitterers who also contribute to Amelia's Magazine. As well as being a laugh I have had the most amazing support from other like-minded lovelies on Twitter. I love the atmosphere: Twitter is the most incredible portal into the illustration world.

Fashion is a massive part of our everyday life.

Yet it's very hard to be completely ethical, so wearing vintage clothing is a really good way of being more sustainable. The Tea and Crayons illustration collective loves vintage fashion so we hope this will inspire many a fantastic project to promote sustainable ideas.

Florence and the Machine craft.

I sell Florence hair pins on Etsy, inspired by an image that I first created for Amelia's Magazine, as well as The Lovely Book of Excuses, a fun handmade zine full of excuses to be used at any time of the day. There is also a selection of cards for tea fans, cake lovers and felt tip dabblers.

Living in Lincoln.

I am currently working part time in a little shop in a little town, which gives me plenty of time to create illustrations for Amelia's Magazine on the side. I intend to take it slowly when it comes to establishing myself in the illustration world because I know it takes five or six years to become well known. Felt tips, tea, it's all good.

Biba A/W 2010

Matthew Innet Graduate Collection

Alice Takes a Trip S/S 2010

BOWS

floral dress

Bobbin Bicycles

Goodone is a tight-knit team who share a passion for sustainable design and fair business practice. At university, designer Nin Castle decided to recycle fabrics as a money saving venture rather than any great interest in sustainability, but after graduating she worked with the cult designer Noki, which compounded her interest in the environmental aspect. **Once I realised how much textile waste is out there it was natural for me to use it.** Since then she has been designing clothes that are either 100% upcycled or incorporate elements of upcycling in the design somewhere. She uses reclaimed industrial waste, including offcuts and faulty fabrics, alongside fabrics manufactured in British mills. **We**

are interested in using new eco fibres in the future, but these will probably need to be sourced abroad.

Goodone has become known for its body-con knitted dresses but there is plenty more in the pipeline. Nin takes fashion trends into consideration when designing **because that's the nature of the beast.** To make an impact on an industry with very well established ideas of pace and schedules it is important to work with what people expect, then there is more opportunity to influence them. ASOS bought her A/W 2009 collection, for which she made some special colourways, and she has also done a range for Topshop. She believes in working with big companies,

Goodone

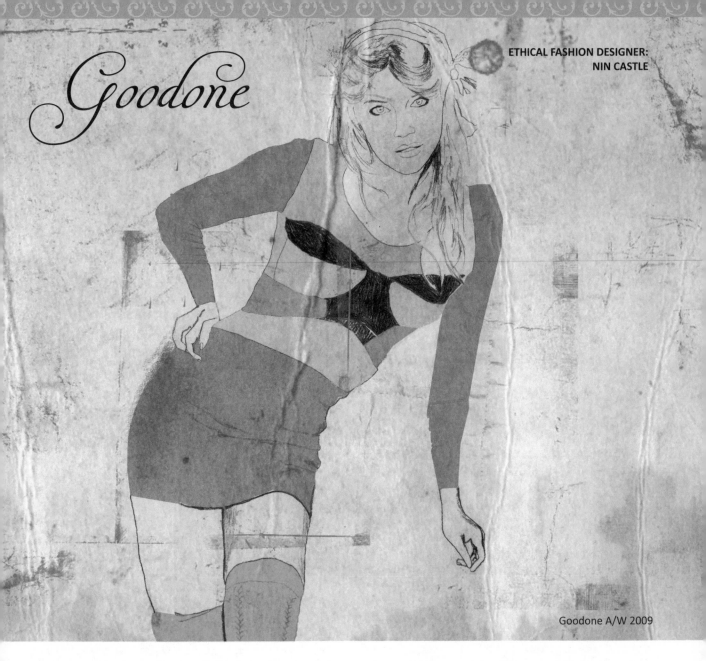

Goodone A/W 2009

not against them. **There is no point in standing on the side lines shouting about how things should be done. It's much better to roll your sleeves up, jump in and see what is possible.**

Nin thinks it is important for people to see sustainable fashion in mainstream shops where it will reach a much wider audience. **Flexibility makes more things possible.** A customer that buys Goodone in Topshop will do so simply because they like the designs, and that's real progress. Once ethical fashion is 'normalised' then it will lose its 'eco' stigma. For the same reason Goodone consult with Tesco. **Like it or not they aren't going anywhere, so**

we are really happy to help them reduce their environmental impact.** Nin also leads workshops at universities as well as sewing classes to teach the general public how to make creative alterations.

As long as we produce new clothing there will be waste to make use of. There is a massive amount of textile waste abroad, and a lot of excess fabric is still burnt. But Nin thinks that companies are slowly realising that it makes sense to waste less because it saves them money in the long run. Upcycling waste to make it more valuable keeps her inspired. **Think creatively, think positively and try to keep a sense of humour.**

Zarina Liew

Why did you chose the name Cobalt Café?

I came up with the idea while visiting my younger sister years ago in Leeds. We visited this amazing Lebanese cafe, filled with the strong scent of mint tea and baklavas, walls washed in a deep cobalt blue. I felt really at home, so when I started illustrating and had to chose a website name, I thought it would recreate that same sense of warmth and visual comfort. I'm also a bit of a foodie and high tea obsessive, so you could say that Cobalt Café reflects my love of cakes as well as art.

You used to work in the city but decided to pursue a career as an artist. What prompted this drastic move?

I never really had any drive or ambition when I was working in the city. I lived for the weekends and enjoyed London for what it was, but I started to feel as if something was missing. I remembered my childhood love of drawing but never thought a career in illustration could be possible until I was kindly prompted by my then colleagues to upload some sketches onto a free online portfolio and within a week I was contacted by BBC Worldwide to draw for some of their magazines. I was shocked but after a couple of commissions I knew that I would have to quit my job, move back to my parents' house and concentrate on drawing again.

How did you teach yourself to draw?

I started to draw anything and everything - badly! I did a lot of research on the artists that I loved and bought a lot of reference books on lighting, painting techniques, and colour mixing. I also enrolled in local life drawing classes; I tried everything to understand my style. I was also fortunate enough to be mentored by a former Central Saint Martin's lecturer and he really helped me develop my drawing. I'm still learning, and I'm always looking for more ways to improve and sharpen my illustrations.

What are your inspirations?

I grew up reading a lot of Manga and I think that my love and appreciation for Eastern art has stemmed from this early childhood habit. I love the simplicity of Japanese art, architecture and fashion design – the subtlety, storytelling and hidden meanings in Japanese art inspire me to create light and emotive work. I also find a lot of inspiration in early British illustration: from Hogarth and Aubrey Beardsley to the gift book illustrators of the early 20th century such as Kay Nielsen and Edmund Dulac – their work is so timeless, skilful and beautiful. I'm a big collector and I am always on the lookout for new styles in illustration. I often attend London arts and craft fairs and press events to meet new artists and illustrators and to buy work that I love and admire. It helps me to understand the current market, appreciate my fellow illustrators and take inspiration for my own work. I also meet up with other artists on a regular basis to share our work and discuss ways in which we can improve and challenge each other. Having a close network of friends in the business has helped me to see things differently and it fuels my passion to create illustrations.

How did your recent collaboration with Nicola Woods come about?

I love the way that Nicola Woods combines oriental and vintage style in her designs so I approached her to see whether she would be happy for me to illustrate Beautiful Soul for this very book. She was so delighted with my artwork that she asked me if I would like to collaborate with her on her S/S 2011 video and lookbook. Of course I said yes! The video was made in three stages – the physical shooting of the models, stop-motion shooting of my work and compiling the two together. I worked with Nicola and her team to create a mood board and mock-up of the scenes involved, then I came in for two days to paint the background. It was a lengthy process because I had to stop 600 times per painting so that the camera could take each shot for the animation but the final outcome is brilliant. You can also see my original artwork for the open brief on her website.

How does your fashion illustration fit in alongside your comic book art?

Conceptual art has a blurry outline and for me, comic art and illustration are very similar. I always try to tell a story in my work; to evoke certain feelings through the characters' clothing and the world they live in. I feel that fashion illustration is just an extension of my comic book art - and vice versa. They exist quite happily alongside each other, and eventually I plan to marry the two themes – so watch this space!

How has appearing in Amelia's Magazine helped to build your career?

Appearing in Amelia's Magazine has allowed my work and reputation to reach that much further, both globally and locally, in a way that would never have been possible before. I have met other inspiring illustrators with whom to share and discuss my artwork, and my love of fashion illustration has been further cemented – I feel fortunate to have been given a lot of support from Amelia's Magazine because it has really boosted my confidence.

What does your studio in west London look like?

My home studio is pretty basic. I have a large table for my scanners, printers and computer as well as three drawer units full of watercolour paper, my inks, paint brushes, art pots, colour markers, pencils, you name it, everything except for the kitchen sink! Actually, I have a small container by the kitchen sink for soaking brushes and cleaning out ink pots. I'm not a very tidy person when it comes to my art so I have a lot of junk on my desk. I collect reference books and scrapbooks as well, so I have these piled up on my drawer units. I used to feel really self-conscious when people came to visit, so I would try to cover my work and hide the evidence, but now I don't mind. It's all out, messy like it should be. The one thing that is important to me is that I sit facing a window and that there is a lot of light coming in. Light is so important - I couldn't work without windows.

Beautiful Soul A/W 2010

self-portrait

What kind of things have you self published?

I run a small zine called The Art of Sleep, which is coming up to its fifth volume now: it's a mixture of comic art and illustrations centred around quirky sleeping habits. I also self-publish a small booklet about my favourite mime artist Le Mime, and at last he's getting a nice amount of interest. I also sell a lot of postcards and greeting cards. I've been featured in the Alternative Press's Publish You compendium and I will shortly be releasing a graphic novel written by fellow small-presser Richy K Chandler (Tempo Lush) called Rosie & Jacinda, a classic, high-school romance story with a lot of kooky characters.

You've been involved in loads of exhibitions, what has been the best way to get these?

The best advice I can give is to start local and start small – find out whether there are any cafes or restaurants in your area that exhibit

Hermione de Paula S/S 2011

artworks and ask them if they would consider your work. You can also pool together an exhibition with other artists at a reasonable price, then invite influential people to spread the word. If you put yourself out there and get to know people in the industry, you'll always be presented with opportunities to exhibit or be commissioned.

What advice would you give anyone in a similar position to you - working in a job they don't want to do but wondering whether they should give it up and risk everything to be an artist?

I think it's important to know exactly what you want and what you're looking for in your art. Being an artist and developing your trade takes years, not to mention a lot of time and effort. I'm comfortable where I am now and I feel that I'm in a fortunate position, but I have spent a lot of time indoors - painting, researching and growing my business. If you are fully committed you will have to make sacrifices and sometimes these are the very little things – not being able to meet friends as often as you'd like, not being able to spend time with your family and not even having enough money to last you through the month. But if you know what you have to do, and you love what you are doing, then your family and friends will understand. Work hard, ask for advice, don't be shy and don't feel daunted. It's lovely to live life knowing you're doing what you love.

How can illustration inspire people to live with more care for the world?

Illustration is an important visual tool that has the power to say so much, more quickly and effectively then a paragraph or sentence. Illustration also transcends culture and nationality, one image may be understood by two people from opposite poles, message received – it's that simple. If you can inspire people through your art and illustration you can educate people into so much more than just thinking "that's a pretty picture".

Beautiful Soul A/W 2010

Bora Aksu A/W 2010

Beautiful Soul S/S 2011

You started out as an insurance broker so you've have had an unconventional career so far. Why and how did you become a fashion designer?

As a young girl, I wanted to be a fashion designer, but life has its twists and turns and I found myself caught up in the rat race for eleven years. I lacked passion for my work but I didn't know how I would cope without my luxuries and the next pay rise. Then I had the opportunity to backpack around the world for six months with my best friend and for the first time in my adult life I realised that I could live on a budget. I started to see life in a different light, with endless opportunities. Whilst in Tokyo, something happened to me: I was surrounded by the most amazing boutiques and I was like a child in a sweet shop. Mesmerised. Excited. Totally inspired. I realised that I needed to make radical changes to my lifestyle in order to make my dreams a reality and I haven't looked back since. I graduated from the London College of Fashion with a BA(Hons) in Fashion, Design and Technology in 2008. During my final year, I was involved in a project based around 'saving the earth'. I was hooked. Fashion with a TRUE meaning, for me, is the only way, and my ethos helps me to focus and push forward.

Why did you decide to specialise in creating adjustable garments?

I set out to create timeless designs that will be favoured pieces in the wardrobe for a lifetime and multi-functionality renders a garment timeless, as it can be worn to suit different moods and seasons. A woman's curves change regularly and it's frustrating when a zip or button will not close. I therefore avoid using conventional fastening in my designs and instead explore alternative methods. I love to experiment and delve below the surface of fashion, discovering new ways to incorporate responsibility through use of distinctive materials and design innovation.

What does your zero waste policy mean in practicality?

I am extremely fond of fabric and I hate to see it go to waste! I upcycle vintage kimonos to create new garments that hold a greater value; when I dismantle a kimono I am left with very limited panels of fabric, only 38cm wide. It's important that I work with these restrictions and nurture an understanding of the fabric availability. Any leftover fabric will be placed aside and then revisited the following season, where I set myself the challenge of designing a new piece based on the leftovers. I have just designed

Beautiful Soul's third collection, S/S 2011's Believe, and the leftover fabrics have been transformed into a range of unique corsets and shoulders pads in our menswear jackets. Material remnants feature as fastenings and embellishments, adhering to the policy of zero waste whereby every last thread of fabric is used in the creative process.

Can you describe your involvement with the Tabeisa charity?

Through the Centre for Sustainable Fashion I won a scholarship to create a sustainable design for which the Tabeisa cooperative in Durban, South Africa could take full ownership. It soon became apparent that a clothing range was out of the question, but with no equipment, masses of ingenuity and all hands on deck, I created a collection using colourful, knotted strings. This was the best work experience I could have hoped for and it sparked my determination to set up my own sustainable fashion label. Beautiful Soul was born upon my return in November 2008.

What was the process of designing your most recent S/S 2011 collection?

Believe is Beautiful Soul's third collection and came to life at our new studio in London's Notting Hill. It has made such a difference to have a proper workstation where everything has a home. I am very open-minded toward design and really listen in order to evolve, so each season I push personal boundaries and set myself new challenges: in addition to the upcycled kimono range, I have developed a Ready to Wear line which features a retro bird print on organic luxury fabrics. The print allows for wholesale orders but sits comfortably alongside the rest of our exclusive designs. I have also introduced a menswear collection: a capsule range of casual blazers made from both upcycled vintage kimonos and the retro bird print featured in the womenswear collection.

What prompted the decision to start printing your own textiles?

The bespoke nature of the upcycled pieces is favoured by clients and stockists who seek individuality. I have learnt however, that many buyers are not able to commit to 'one of a kind' pieces, despite their creative appeal. They cannot take the risk of confusing their customers. I have therefore introduced a retro print collaboration with Polly Hope, an eco textiles designer. The print allows for wholesale orders but sits comfortably alongside the rest of the brand's exclusive designs. Polly Hope and I met last year at the Ethical Fashion Forum's Marketplace and we have stayed in touch ever since. She creates textiles using organic fabrics and herbal dyes; ensuring fairtrade standards and a chemical-free work place.

Why did you decide to move into menswear as well?

On several occasions I was asked to make bespoke pieces for male friends and I discovered that the vintage kimonos work well as outerwear and transformed into blazers. There seems to be a lack of eco-aware menswear currently available, so we will develop Beautiful Soul's offering each season to provide a range that compliments our womens-wear collection and ethos.

Your latest video collaboration with Zarina Liew was prompted by the open brief for this book. How did it come about?

Zarina Liew contacted me in response to the Amelia's Magazine open brief and I immediately fell in love with her work so we hit it off straight away. Having only recently set up my fashion label I am constantly juggling finances to find creative solutions and my budget will not yet stretch to a fashion show. Film seemed to be the perfect solution; from the outset, I wanted to make a positive, creative short film that would celebrate the energy of Beautiful Soul and my ideas evolved. Eventually I drew a team of creatives together that included Zarina, photographer Oliver Prout and stylist Rivkie Baum and we are all equally responsible for the final film.

Can you describe the process for producing it?

I had to be extremely resourceful; it took several weeks to put together the team and produce the film. It was filmed in the empty studio across the hallway and we created our own green screen studio against which we shot the models and took stills for my lookbook. It was the first time I'd seen my collection in motion and it was an amazing feeling to see it come to life after months of hard work. We then worked through the night to create stop motion animations of Zarina's drawings and Oliver translated the final footage into Beautiful Soul's first fashion film. He even made a short film to document the journey.

What is the best way to care for our planet?

Use common sense. Our planet has been around a lot longer than we humans and will continue without us. Show respect and preserve it. Caring for the planet is not a trend, it is the only way forward. Once I have built a steady foundation for Beautiful Soul, I hope to share my skills and inspire the next generation of designers to think positively and compassionately about the world we live in.

Beautiful Soul A/W 2010

Maison Martin Margiela

Bora Aksu for People Tree

Beautiful Soul A/W 2010

Joana Faria

FASHION ILLUSTRATOR

self-portrait

Brazilian illustrator Joana Faria studied in London and is now settled in Portugal, where the discovery of Amelia's Magazine has brought a renewed vigour to her love of drawing.

Why do you like to draw cute girls?
I've always drawn girls in dresses and skirts with flowers in their hair. I guess the child in me takes over when I start drawing and all my girls have very long necks, big hair and huge eyes. The eyes are my favourite part to draw. Maybe that's why I make them so big, so they will take me longer to finish.

How do you create your fashion illustrations?
My process is usually very simple: if there's a piece of paper and a black marker nearby, I'll start drawing. I'm quite instinctive and I don't really plan my compositions, but if I am drawing a particular dress or accessory then I focus on that and work around it, putting in as many details as possible: I find filling the page with patterns almost therapeutic and it completely relaxes me. If other people are going to take their time to pay attention to my images I feel that I have a responsibility to make them beautiful. In the end I believe that when you put some love into your work it really shows.

How have your Brazilian roots affected your approach to illustration?
Although I grew up in London during my teens, I was born in Brazil and spent my whole childhood there. As a child I had a very close group of girlfriends, who to this day are still my best friends. I would make little portraits of them that included something of their character and I think that's why I'm always drawing girls. I guess I miss my friends and my girls are a way to recreate them on paper.

What is it like to be an illustrator in Portugal?
Portugal is beautiful and there's plenty of inspiration all around: the gorgeous patterns in the tiles and mosaics, the pastel colours of the houses in Lisbon, and everywhere the amazing light. Everything is worthy of observation and there is something pretty to find everyday. There are some brilliant illustrators here but the scene is very small, as is the potential market for illustration - it doesn't compare to London or São Paolo. There are a lot more opportunities in the UK.

Why did you decide to turn your hand to illustration?
I studied photography at Goldsmiths College in London and have been working as a creative in advertising agencies both in London and in Portugal ever since I graduated from university, but illustration has always been at the back of my mind and every day that goes by I love it more. I was browsing online when I found Amelia's Magazine, and something just clicked: I realised that I could create illustrations from anywhere in the world.

How has being an art director helped your illustration?
Being an art director in advertising agencies has taught me to think of everything in visual terms. An advert, a certain scene in a film, a shop window; everything communicates to us visually. Being aware of this helps me to build the colour, lines and textures of my compositions. And I am not afraid to experiment and try new things.

What has happened since you started using social networks?
Twitter has been great. It has allowed me to get to know other illustrators that are just starting out like me, and it has also helped me to get involved in illustration competitions and assignments that I would otherwise never have known about. I saw a post from Hello You Creatives on Twitter asking for illustrators to submit work for their newspaper and one of my pieces was published! It was really tiny, but it felt good to be recognised and know that there are people out there who like the work I'm doing. I feel much more part of the creative community now.

What is the market for ethical fashion in Portugal?
I had honestly never heard of ethical fashion before I read about this book, and I love the idea. Fashion designers in general have a very strong presence and influence in our lives. We observe what they do and we listen to what they have to say. Ethical fashion designers are able to use that influence more wisely. They can inspire us to pay attention, understand how fashion can help reduce poverty and protect the environment... and make good choices that are not based only on beauty or trends.

Apartment C A/W 2010

PARTIMI S/S 2011
Dieu Bleu

Apartment C A/W 2010

Apartment C A/W 2010

Aqua by Aqua A/W 2010

Emma Ware

Jewellery from tyres.

I have always been attracted to colourful, shiny, fun pieces of old broken jewellery, toys and bottle tops; stuff that others would consider rubbish or of no use. It doesn't make ecological or economic sense to manufacture new materials when there is so much out there already. Reusing materials changes the way you design because it forces you to work within the limits of the material you have and I am constantly on the lookout for new waste materials to use. One day my friend had a puncture, and seeing potential in the rubber ring of the inner tube I had a go at chopping it up and immediately knew I was onto something.

Elegance in rubber.

I create designs based on what the rubber wants me to do, playing with the natural shapes when it is cut up in different ways. Making repetitive cuts in graduated sizes of inner tubes rings seems to result in designs that imitate naturally occurring organic patterns; similar to those found in wings, feathers, leaves, shells or even waves. My signature pieces are based on cutting the tube in a specific way, from which I figure out how I can make something to complement the human form.

Scouting for materials.

I collect bicycle tubes from my local bike shops but I am often in competition with the scouts who do their best to beat me to the tubes. There's an incredible range of shapes and sizes to sort through, and each is particularly good for a specific design. I wash them, paint them, slice them up, stitch them together and/or thread them onto a chain. I often come across a beautiful new form when I am trying to reproduce a previous design, so I have a lot of random shapes hanging around, just waiting for the right moment to be transformed into a final piece of jewellery.

Juggling careers.

Occasionally I also work as a camera assistant, which I find works well with jewellery making because it is so different. Most of the time I concentrate on making my jewellery but I also paint and take photos, both of which I hope to do more of in the future. With my camera skills I was able to make a promotional film for my accessories.

Sustainability at home.

Everything I do is informed by a respect for nature and the environment. My dream is to be self sufficient, maybe in the countryside, but at the moment I'm very far away from that. Right now I seem to be a city girl so I do what I can: growing vegetables, recycling and reusing, using products that don't pollute, buying local and cycling as much as possible. It's important to find a balance, because it's easy to get stressed-out worrying over the effect of every single action, and that doesn't help anything.

Prangsta Costumiers

Romina Karamanea S/S 2011

Zandra Rhodes

We take amazing fashion photography for granted... but a fashion illustration can really capture the imagination. It's a special privilege to take a fashion designer's creation and work with it as part of my own creative process, but sometimes I get carried away with my own ideas so I have to try and remember that capturing the essence of the clothing is the most important thing - I always hope that the designer will like what I do. **Fashion illustration requires me to rein in my wilder flights of fancy.** For my portrait I wear my dream dress by Issey Miyake; owning this dress would be akin to wearing an amazing piece of art.

I was first attracted to Christopher Raeburn's clothes because of their wonderful translucent jellyfish-like quality, so I styled his creations with highly coloured and patterned garments underneath. I am a big fan of vintage clothes and I love the idea that his fabric has had a previous life as parachutes and other military paraphernalia. **Where I live in Scotland it's always rainy and his coats would be perfect for me; I could wear a really nice printed dress beneath.** To create my illustrations I build up layers of cut paper shapes on the scanner and for Christopher Raeburn's designs I used lots of transparent film, coloured acetate and tracing paper, mixing the colours to create a kaleidoscope effect.

Creating the endpapers for Amelia's Anthology of Illustration got me over my fear of colour. Before that I was intimidated by colour so I did most of my work in monochrome but nowadays I have to restrain myself from using too many colours at once. Amelia's Magazine online has allowed me to tackle fashion illustration briefs for the first time, helping me to

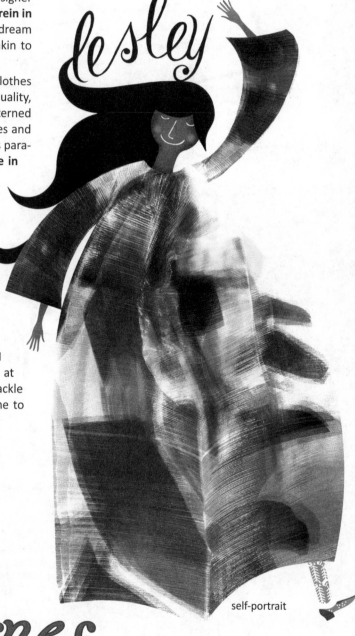

self-portrait

Lesley Barnes

develop my work and see how other illustrators tackle the same designers. Other projects I am working on include the promotional material for jazz musician Kit Downes. We are about to start work on a collaborative performance of music and animation.

I love Twitter. **I have met so many other talented illustrators through Twitter, many of whom I have also met in 'real life' as well.** Together we have started a number of projects which I don't think would ever have got off the ground before. I met the lovely Thereza Rowe through Amelia's Magazine and then on Twitter, and we collaborated together on an animation for a Sesame Street competition. Twitter is especially good for people who work from home because it's an easy way to chat with other freelancers.

In my humble opinion HRH is a style icon who must surely have one of the finest 'old lady' hat collections in the world... does she ever wear the same hat twice? Where do her retired hats go? Maybe you can unwittingly pick one up in Oxfam? In my mind she has a special hat room where she stores each hat by colour and by date or perhaps event... maybe even mood? **I am determined to create an illustrated guide to the Queen and her Hats** – I feel as though it is essential that someone catalogues them.

There are lots of nice things about working from home but it can get lonely so ultimately I would like to share my studio and tea-making facilities with other people. In the next ten years I would hope to be making a good living doing what I love. **My ideal studio space would be in a library in a castle; a room with thick walls and high ceilings.** I would be surrounded by piles and piles of books, prints, artwork by my friends and strange objects from my travels. I like to be cocooned by inspiring things and bright colours. I spend my days listening to BBC 6 Music and of course because I live in Glasgow I only play Belle and Sebastian (I designed a t-shirt for them recently) and a little vintage Orange Juice. I also love the new Edwyn Collins album.

I am a self taught illustrator so I missed out on a lot of things, but this has probably helped me to develop my own style because I haven't been influenced by tutors or classmates. Although I have a lot to learn, my best advice to aspiring creatives is **get online and get your work out there**. If nobody sees it then you won't get commissions. Of course I sometimes look at the work of other illustrators and think, 'why can't I be more like them?' but it's best to create a unique style rather than simply following illustration trends.

RCA MA Graduate Collection 2010

Holly Fulton S/S 2011

Lu Flux S/S 2011

ETHICAL FASHION DESIGNER

Lu Flux was borne Elizabeth Flux, but gained her delightful moniker thanks to her little brother's inability to say her full name. She hails from the Isle of Wight, "a very lovely quintessentially English part of the UK" and she designs against the grain of glamorous fashion, making eccentric playfulness desirable.

How much did working with Bernard Wilhelm affect your aesthetic?

I was interested in the wonderful silliness of fashion before I went to work with Bernhard, but he reaffirmed to me that it is possible to have a successful fashion label without a focal point of glamour and sex. For me fashion is a tool with which I can portray fun and humour in a beautifully crafted, wearable way.

What is the most exciting bit of fabric you have come across on your hunt for treasures?

There are so many! I really enjoy finding old patchwork quilts and samplers where the fabrics have faded over time. I have devoted a whole wall of my studio to floral cottons, so I am quite spoilt for choice yet there is always room for a few more...

How do you set about creating your more sculptural pieces?

I normally start out by doing some experiments and manipulations with fabrics to see what works on different scales with different weights of fabric. Then I do some more studies and drawings of the fabric until I feel it will work within a garment. Lastly I construct a demonstration version of the garment (a toile) until I feel it is right.

Why is it important for you to be ethical?

I think it is important for everyone to be ethical, in every aspect of life. I don't think that I can save the world with what I am doing, but I believe that if everyone worked and lived in a more ethical way the world would not be in the state it is in now. In regards to fashion, I passionately believe that a garment can be both beautiful and ecologically minded. I will always retain my original aim to design and manufacture fashion in a way that recognises its imprint on society and the environment but I would not like this ethos to distract from my capabilities as a designer.

Why is it more rewarding to be ethical?

My collections revolve around the vintage and salvaged materials that I find by working with recycling companies. It is satisfying and fulfilling to address the disposable side of the fashion industry by making something new out of something old. My designs are spawned by the fabrics that I find and the desire to make clothes that are fun, individual and beautiful.

Who do you regularly collaborate with?

Since we met at Edinburgh College of Art the artist Neil O'Driscoll and I have worked together a lot. We share the same vision and he has directed all of the films made to accompany the collections, including The Eco Life of Riley for S/S 2010, which was filmed in Epping Forest on a Super 8 camera. Films can portray a really good mood for a collection, creating a story without needing to accurately document the clothes. Neil also provided the illustrations for a bespoke Lu Flux Toile de Jouy fabric in my S/S 2011 collection Over the Hills and Far Away, and at my presentation he did some live artwork. I work with some incredibly talented people who add an extra dimension to my designs that I could not achieve alone. Keep your eyes peeled for some more collaborations.

Do you think there will be a catwalk show next year, and if so what can we expect?

Presentations are a lot of hard work but great fun to put together and I like mingling with the audience. It will be a few more seasons before I do a catwalk show because I still have some great ideas for presentations. And I don't think I am ready just yet.

How did you set about working with SOKO Kenya, a sustainable grassroots workshop?

I am a member of the Ethical Fashion Forum so they were able to help me out when I wanted to do a community-based project. It was quite hard to get the designs right because all correspondence was via email so samples and swatches were viewed as photos only. Each piece was handmade by a different person so the end results were all quirkily unique.

Can we expect any more collaborations with Green Shoes?

Of course! I love working with Green Shoes - the team is great and they have such a wide choice of eco-tan leathers to choose from. All my shoes and bags are hand made to order but sometimes my shoe designs are slightly off the wall so we have to tone them down to work as functional footwear.

You don't really work with fashion trends - is this ever a problem in selling clothes?

I am getting much more aware of the pieces that are likely to sell as each season comes and goes. I am also gathering a loyal following of customers from all over the world who understand my ethos - which is fantastic. I just need to keep plugging away little by little. It can be difficult because a lot of my pieces are one-offs due to my use of vintage fabrics, so in production we make sure we retain the colour palette of a pattern even if the specific fabrics change.

What do you do to recharge your batteries?

Whenever I need to escape I go to the Isle of Wight with my boyfriend Alex and our Bearded Collie Burt Wellington. I have to exercise Burt twice a day which is great because it means that I am able to get out of the studio, stretch my legs and muse over what I am doing, then I return refreshed and ready to go again. Sometimes we take Burt to Epping Forest or Whipps Cross where there is a boating lake he likes to paddle in. I also like getting out of London to go to car boot sales and jumble sales.

What will you be doing in ten years time?

I hope to be living in the country with Alex and Burt - perhaps on the Isle of Wight - still designing, still making and perhaps with a couple of kiddies running around too. Am I asking too much?

Little Glass Clementine

Why the name?

I made up the name when I was at my family home on the Mull of Kintyre in Scotland, where I collect endless pieces of sea polished glass from the beach. I combined that with my first name Clementine because I thought it was kind of sweet.

Where do you work from?

I used to live and work on a little leaking narrow boat by Springfield Park in north London. But I now have a proper studio in Dalston with a big work desk. Makes life a little easier - less rocking!

You aren't a trained jewellery designer, so what prompted you to start Little Glass Clementine?

ETHICAL JEWELLERY DESIGNER: CLEMENTINE JAMES

Little Glass Clementine S/S 2011

I taught myself to make jewellery so that I could support myself through my degree at SOAS, where I studied Anthropology and World Religions, and I ran stalls at the markets in Portobello and Camden for the best part of three years. Then I became busy restoring gypsy caravans and being a climate activist, but now I am in love with the discovery of beautiful antiques and unusual stones that I transform into sculptural necklaces. I quickly realised that my market is high-end, where my statement necklaces will be recognised as art.

How does showing at Estethica compare with working on a market stall?

It's a bit like being back in the market, bantering with passers by, drinking coffee and chatting about my jewels. But with a few distinctive differences; there is no reggae playing, I'm not freezing cold, and my prices and pieces have changed - quite dramatically.

How do you put each necklace together?

I arrange all the components on an old piece of black velvet, making compositions out of the different objects and gems until I am satisfied. Then I start weaving them all together and hope very much I can recreate what I had when I laid them out. I only use wire and I never glue or make holes in the objects - so there is always a period while I'm working where everything looks like a big entangled mess. Strangely enough I am never convinced that a necklace is right until about five minutes before it is finished - when suddenly one stone, broach or button will bring the whole thing together.

How do you work on a private commission and what has been your most memorable job?

My client will come to a meeting with a few special pieces of sentimental value that are to be incorporated into a necklace. Then we go through my boxes of broken jewellery, old strings of gems, antiques and organic treasures, placing everything on the black velvet to see what composition we like. I made a necklace for a bride which included treasures from four generations of women: a piece of silk lace from her great grandmother's wedding dress, earrings from her grandmother, a brooch from her mother and some stones from a broken necklace belonging to the bride. It was truly gorgeous.

Why is a narrative so important to the creation of your necklaces?

When I was very young I had to write a story about the journey of a £1 coin, and since then I have been fascinated by the stories behind an object. I always wonder why something has been discarded. Why was this ring no longer worn? Was this piece of lace made by a girl who was sitting with friends, chatting, while she made it? How long was this pebble on a beach, and was it once on the bottom of the sea? I believe my necklaces are full of secret narratives that will engage people in different ways.

Why do you like to run skill share workshops?

I believe that in general people need to share their skills more, so it is always a pleasure to pass on mine at upcycling workshops. I ask participants to bring along a few of their own pieces to work into their necklace and then show them how to weave everything together with wire. Because I am self taught my technique is easy to pick up. Prince Charles came to one of my workshops at the Garden Party during London Fashion Week. He particularly liked the necklace I made out of a bath plug, and said I was "jolly clever" in a very posh voice.

In 2009 you visited Tuvalu to raise awareness of the effects of climate change - how does this trip continue to impact the way that you work?

Climate change is a reality that increasingly my generation will have to deal with. I started Climate Friend as a way for young people in Tuvalu, Bangladesh and Britain to communicate ideas about climate change through emails, letters and art. The youth need to be able to speak for themselves so I often hold Climate Friend workshops at climate change conferences. I feel it's important to take direct action in order to highlight the effects of climate change, but the reality is that people will always adorn themselves. Trying to change the world does not also equate to be boring in what we wear. I think that creating Little Glass Clementine is part of being an activist: it is important to show that we can adorn ourselves in sustainable and ethical ways.

What are you thoughts on the fashion industry in general?

I think the fashion world is unsustainable - it needs to slow down and change on a dramatic scale, but for that to happen it's important to provide an alternative. I make gorgeous recycled and reclaimed necklaces that show it is possible to dress with style without exploiting resources on our finite planet, because the earth cannot keep up with our current demands. The reality of fast fashion means that somewhere along the production line something is being exploited, whether that be natural resources or a human worker. I believe we will all become more creative in the coming years. We will see smaller fashion houses and more focus on craft and cottage industries. This is an exciting time, not one of doom. There are thousands of materials out there just begging to be refashioned.

Hiroaki Ohya

Emma Box Graduate Collection 2010

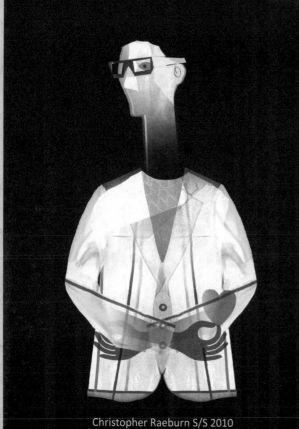

Christopher Raeburn S/S 2010

Betty Jackson S/S 2011

Christopher Raeburn S/S 2010

Hetty Rose

You make bespoke shoes... if I wanted a pair of shoes for myself how would the process work?

I create a collection each season from which clients can choose a design, then they decide which vintage Japanese kimono fabric they would like their shoes made up in. Clients can alter the shape and height of the heel so that the shoes are totally unique to them. I usually meet them personally if they are UK based, and we have tea whilst I measure their feet and bring them fabric samples to muse through. It's a very interactive purchase, with the client involved in every step of the design because I want them to have an emotional attachment to the shoes so that they will treasure them and love wearing them. I email them photos during the process of making the shoes so they can see them being created. At the halfway point they are ready for a fitting and after that I finish off the sole and attach the heels. The whole process takes around six to eight weeks and prices start from £350. With international clients everything is done via email - it's exciting for them to receive a pair of shoes all the way from a little workshop in England.

How else can someone get a pair of your shoes?

Following increased sales and press attention we have decided to extend the Hetty Rose brand to a wider audience, who will be able to own a precious piece of designer footwear at a more affordable price point and without the long wait for a pair of bespoke shoes. Our Ready to Wear collection features some of our best selling styles in kimono fabrics, and can be bought directly from our website. In the future I plan to add more accessories such as bags, baby shoes, homewares and ties for men.

You use vintage Japanese kimono fabrics to make your shoes, but what else are they made of?

All the components I use are as sustainable as possible. I reuse some leathers from vintage jackets and trousers, and the insoles of the shoes are made from recycled materials. For a recent collection we used antique brooches and vintage materials found at flea markets. We also encourage clients to bring

Nowadays I have a few good suppliers who know my taste but I go back to Japan as often as I can. I love to create something amazing from fabrics which would otherwise be forgotten. Over the years I have tested many ways of making the fabrics strong enough for shoes and I now add a cotton back to the silks, which makes them strong enough to be durable, yet flexible enough to mould around the last (the form on which I make the shoes).

Why are you based in Essex?

I often have to go into London to visit clients or to source materials, but rents are too high for a decent sized studio space and I would get distracted by so much going on. Hence I prefer to be out in Essex in a huge workspace where I can concentrate really well. The studio is where my ideas come together and I love to be immersed in shoe making: I have a big work table on top of which sits an industrial sewing machine that I inherited from my grandmother, and around me are stacks of sample shoes, fabrics, leathers and other components.

Why do you get involved in so many collaborative projects?

I get bored easily so I am known for doing lots of things all the time. I meet lots of interesting people through my work and this sometimes leads to working on projects together. For instance with an art student I created a fun little animation to demonstrate how my shoes are made. My mother loves the work of William Morris, so I visited the gallery and applied for a place in their next exhibition. As a result I made a collection of shoes that used Morris inspired prints and my mum got to attend the private view. I like being involved in different projects, it means I can try out unusual ideas and that keeps my creativity fresh.

us their coveted trinkets to include in their shoe's design, thus making them wearable once again rather than forlornly stuck in a jewellery box for years. We have recycling sections in the workshop to make sure we reuse as much as we can - for example offcuts are used in the making of purses. We hold an environmental audit certification for the workshop.

What made you decide to work with kimono fabrics?

I was travelling in Japan several years ago when I chanced across lots of small shops that were selling traditional kimono fabrics, and I realised that the panels of fabric lent themselves perfectly to the width of a shoe pattern. Hence I left all my clothes in Japan and filled my suitcases with these fabrics.

Christopher Raeburn

Online Fashion Illustrators

Abby Wright
www.abbywrightillustration.co.uk
twitter.com/abbyillustrator

Abigail Daker
www.abigaildaker.com
twitter.com/abigaildaker

Amy Martino
www.yellowbirdmachine.com
twitter.com/amybirdmachine

Andrea Peterson
www.artistandrea.com
twitter.com/ArtistAndrea

Aniela Murphy
www.anielamurphy.co.uk
twitter.com/AnielaMurphy

Antonia Parker
www.antoniamakes.com
twitter.com/antoniamakes

Bex Glover
www.severnstudios.co.uk
twitter.com/SevernStudios

Emma Block
www.emmablock.co.uk
twitter.com/EmmaBlock

Erica Sharp
www.ericasharp.co.uk
twitter.com/erica_sharp

Faye West
www.fayewest.com
twitter.com/westfaye

Gareth A Hopkins
www.grthink.com
twitter.com/grthink

Gemma Milly
www.gemmamilly.com
twitter.com/GemmaMillie

Jenny Costello
www.jenillustration.com
twitter.com/jenillustration

Jenny Robins
www.jennyrobins.co.uk
twitter.com/jennyrobins

Jo Cheung
www.jocheung.com
twitter.com/jocheung

Joana Faria
www.atelierjoanafaria.com
twitter.com/joana_faria

June Chanpoomidole
www.junesees.com
twitter.com/junesees

Katherine Tromans
www.katherinetromans.com
twitter.com/kattromans

Katie Harnett
www.katieharnett.com
twitter.com/teabelle

Kellie Black
www.misspearlgrey.com
twitter.com/misspearlgrey

Krister Selin
www.kristerselin.com
twitter.com/KristerSelin

Lesley Barnes
www.lesleybarnes.co.uk
twitter.com/lesleybarnes

Lisa Stannard
www.lisastannard.com
twitter.com/Lisa_Stannard

Michelle Urvall Nyren
www.michelleurvallnyren.com
twitter.com/michelleurvall

Naomi Law
www.nimlawdraws.co.uk
twitter.com/nimlawdraws

Natasha Thompson
www.thesecretteaparty.co.uk
twitter.com/natashalikestea

Natsuki Otani
www.natsukiotani.co.uk
twitter.com/nat_o

Rachel de Ste Croix
www.precious-little.com
twitter.com/precious_little

Yelena Bryksenkova
www.yelenabryksenkova.com
twitter.com/ybryksenkova

Zarina Liew
www.cobaltcafe.co.uk
twitter.com/cobaltcafe

Ethical Fashion Designers

123
www.123bethnalgreenroad.co.uk

Ada Zanditon
www.adaz.co.uk

Andrea Crews
www.andreacrews.com

Anja Hynynen
www.anjahynynen.com

Beautiful Soul
www.beautiful-soul.co.uk

By Stamo
www.stamo.co.uk

Camilla Norrback
www.camillanorrback.com

Christopher Raeburn
www.christopherraeburn.co.uk

Ciel
www.ciel.ltd.uk

Dem Collective
www.demcollective.com

Edun
www.edun.com

Emesha
www.emesha.com

Emma Ware
www.emmaware.co.uk

Fifi Bijoux
www.fifibijoux.com

From Somewhere
www.fromsomewhere.co.uk

Goodone
www.goodone.co.uk

Gossypium
www.gossypium.co.uk

Henrietta Ludgate
www.henriettaludgate.com

Hetty Rose
www.hettyrose.co.uk

Howies
www.howies.co.uk

Ivana Basilotta
www.ivanabasilotta.co.uk

Izzy Lane
www.izzylane.com

Joanna Cave
www.joannacave.com

Junky Styling
www.junkystyling.co.uk

Little Glass Clementine
www.littleglassclementine.co.uk

Lu Flux
www.luflux.com

Martina Spetlova
www.martinaspetlova.com

Maxjenny
www.maxjenny.com

Michelle Lowe-Holder
www.lowe-holder.com

Minna
www.minna.co.uk

Nancy Dee
www.nancydee.co.uk

Nina Dolcetti
www.ninadolcetti.com

Noir
www.noir.dk

Noki
www.novamatic.com

Oria
www.oriajewellery.co.uk

Partimi
www.partimi.com

People Tree
www.peopletree.co.uk

Pia Anjou
www.pianjou.com

Prophetik
www.prophetik.com

Romina Karamanea
www.rominakaramanea.com

Sägen
www.sagenbutik.se

Satoshi Date
www.satoshidate.com

Tara Starlet
www.tarastarlet.com

Ute Decker
www.utedecker.com

Wilfried Pletzinger
www.w-pletzinger.se

This book was published independently by Amelia's House, an offshoot of Amelia's Magazine. The print version of Amelia's Magazine began life in early 2004 but after ten biannual issues it moved entirely online in late 2008. Amelia's Magazine showcases the very best in underground and independent fashion, illustration, art, music and environmental activism.

In late 2009 Amelia's Anthology of Illustration (featuring renewable technologies to prevent catastrophic climate change) was published by Amelia's House. This colourful 264 page hardback book presents the work of forty up and coming illustrators alongside dazzling illustrations and simple explanations of renewable technologies. Purchase Amelia's Anthology of Illustration online at my website, or simply ask for a copy at any good book store.

Praise for Amelia's Anthology of Illustration:

"this is the illustration book I have been waiting for. If you're an illustrator, hell, if you're an artist, image maker or image enthusiast you need to own this book" - **Cheapzine**

"Amelia's Anthology of Illustration looks gorgeous on my coffee table and everyone picks it up to have a peak." - **Creative Boom**

"This is a gorgeous book with a message to spread." - **Pikaland**

"It's a must to have for all people who are into illustration or that just love art." - **Imaginative Bloom**

"Amelia's Anthology of Illustration really is something special... To turn something serious into something beautiful - that's a gift." - **The Playground**

Catch up with Amelia's Magazine and Amelia's House online:

www.ameliasmagazine.com
twitter.com/ameliasmagazine
www.facebook.com/amelias.mag
www.youtube.com/user/ameliashouse